The Greatest Team of All Time

As Selected by Baseball's Immortals, from Ty Cobb to Willie Mays

Compiled by
Nicholas Acocella and Donald Dewey

BOB ADAMS, INC.
Holbrook, Massachusetts

Published by Bob Adams, Inc. 260 Center Street, Holbrook, MA 02343

ISBN: 1-55850-421-4

Printed in the United States of America.

J I H G F E D C B A

Library of Congress Cataloging-in-Publication Data
Acocella, Nick.
The greatest team of all time : as selected by baseball's immortals from Ty Cobb to Willie
Mays / compiled by Nicholas Acocella and Donald Dewey.
p.   cm.
Includes index.
ISBN 1-55850-421-4
1. Baseball players—United States—Rating of. I. Dewey, Donald, 1940–   . II. Title.
GV865.A1A28   1994
796.357'02—dc20   94-31483
                                             CIP

This publication is designed to provide accurate and authoritative information with regard to the subject
matter covered. It is sold with the understanding that the publisher is not engaged in rendering legal, ac-
counting, or other professional advice. If legal advice or other expert assistance is required, the services of
a competent professional person should be sought.
    — From a *Declaration of Principles* jointly adopted by a Committee of the American Bar Association
and a Committee of Publishers and Associations

This book is available at quantity discounts for bulk purchases.
For information, call 1-800-872-5627.

For
Joseph Delaney
and
Ben Acocella

Contents

Hall of Famer Teams

Addendum: Hall of Famers without Lineups

Addendum: Threshold Hall of Famers

Preface

The marketing of nostalgia and fantasy has become as visible a part of baseball as the signing of free agents and the griping from ownership about franchises losing money. Teams hold annual old-timer promotions. All-star old-timers tour major cities for exhibition contests. Franchise after franchise schedules elaborate ceremonies for retiring the uniform number of a former player, even when he may still be active for another club. For thousands of dollars, graying, paunchy fans fly to Florida or Arizona to play on the same field with the diamond heroes of their youth. Baseball card conventions draw thousands of collectors and prompt financial transactions that would make most art collectors blush. Bookstore shelves are laden with reminiscences of sportswriters who covered the Boys of Summer and the rotisserie daydreams of would-be George Steinbrenners. Trade papers print the results of computerized games, played only on a monitor, between Murderers Row and the Big Red Machine.

We have heard, seen, and read about baseball past, present, and nonexistent. Just about everybody has described where he was, when it was, and how it was. Just about everybody.

Except the players themselves.

As clear as the merits of Hank Aaron or Willie Mays may be from a pressbox or the bleachers, no sportswriter or fan has ever had to paint the outside corner against Aaron or has driven Mays to the center field fence for a long out. Even the most assiduous student of box scores would be hard pressed to account for the psychological impact of a player's presence in the lineup, the dugout, or the locker room. Increasingly, statisticians have agreed that batting and fielding averages are insufficient gauges of the talent of a player. But to what extent did the players ever believe in those numbers anyway? Or in the new numbers either, for that matter?

The suggestion here is not that only big league players are in a position to offer expert evaluations of what takes place between the white lines. If personal experience were the only criterion for judging ability, Babe Ruth might have looked at his 14 strikeouts in 25 appearances against Hub Pruett and nominated the 29-48 journeyman for the Hall of Fame, Aaron might count his 17 career home runs against Don Drysdale as 17 reasons for denying the Dodger hurler a place in Cooperstown, and several seasons of New York Yankees might vote for Frank Lary as the greatest pitcher of all time. The point, rather, is that by *excluding* the personal and team experiences of those who have done the actual playing, any perspective on baseball history is a limited one. This book strives to overcome that limitation by providing a forum for the views and unique insights of baseball's best—Hall of Famers and threshold Hall of Famers.

Introduction

The first game in the major leagues as we know them today was played between Boston and Philadelphia on Saturday, April 22, 1876. The last time there was anything approaching unanimity in speculating about the greatest possible all-time all-star baseball team was Sunday, April 23, 1876. In the twelve decades since then, thousands of players have jogged through millions of memories and appreciations of what they did or did not accomplish on the diamond. Some of the players have excited the memory to a legendary degree, to the point where we can recall them in the most characteristic of details despite never having seen them play. Others have kept our attention through argumentative statistics, fortuitous games, and dramatic at bats. The greats are not only the players we saw, but the players we *believe* we saw. We are known as fans—as in fanatic, but also as in fancy.

Every ballplayer is subject to the same temptations and prejudices as the fan sitting in the loge section behind home plate. If he can be assumed to have more of an inside professional perspective, he can likewise be expected to have deeper personal enthusiasms or rancors where his contemporaries are concerned. Also, like the sunbather in the bleachers, the player has grown up within the lore and the myths of the game and perhaps remains even more impressed by a predecessor who once toed the same mound or stood on the same outfield grass. The player-as-fan has his agendas, too.

In compiling *The Greatest Team of All Time* the authors have addressed themselves to the players-as-fans; more specifically, to the best players of all time—Hall of Famers and those standing on the threshold of being honored at Cooperstown. Every player was asked to choose the ideal team he would field if he had to win one big game. The objective was not so much to conduct an election for the theoretically strongest lineup of all time as to record the players' first-hand, knowledgeable evaluations of the different periods in the evolution of twentieth-century baseball. For the most part, *The Greatest Team of All Time* has emerged from personal, written, and telephone interviews conducted specifically for the book. Other lineups were gathered by one or both of the authors in the course of unrelated newspaper or magazine assignments. And a third group of responses—embracing the contributions of legends like Ty Cobb, Sam Crawford, Fred Clarke, Mickey Cochrane, Nap Lajoie, Carl Hubbell, Dazzy Vance, Charlie Gehringer, and Hank Greenberg—goes back more than 30 years when one of the authors, then a teenager, wrote to every member of the Hall of Fame and asked each to pick a personal all-time all-star team.

In asking every player for his lineup, the stipulation was that he confine his choices to one-time teammates and rivals. (The preference for former teammates was particularly blatant among those who played for the Brooklyn Dodgers in the 1950s.) Several players objected to this restriction, however, saying that they were as capable of judging talent from a stadium seat or an armchair in front of a television set as they had been from the dugout. As a result, some lineups span generations, with conspicuous benefit to, among others, Brooks Robinson and Keith Hernandez. Similarly, some players said they would feel uncomfortable leaving out such legends as Babe Ruth and Lou Gehrig, even though they had never seen them play.

Although those responding generally agreed to the ground rule of one player per position, a few indicated that they found it impossible to choose between, say, Juan Marichal and Bob Gibson and asked that the alternative be listed somewhere. Other respondents, among them Ralph Kiner and Roy Campanella, insisted that if they had to win one game, there was no way, even theoretically, that they would leave themselves out of such a lineup.

As interesting as some of the names advanced by the respondents are those not put forward as frequently as one might have expected; falling into this category are, among others, Kiner, Greenberg, Mel Ott, Lefty Gomez, and Pete Rose. The need for defense in a conjectural winner-take-all game also seems to have cost Stan Musial, Ernie Banks, and Harmon Killebrew, yet raised the value of non-Hall of Famers like Gil Hodges and Vic Power.

In follow-up questions about whom they considered their most difficult one-on-one nemesis and the most under rated player from their era, the names Ewell Blackwell and Ken Keltner cropped up more than once. A number of players were also emphatic on the point that the home run feats of Hank Aaron and Roger Maris obscured their all-around offensive and defensive brilliance and made them appear more one-dimensional than was the case.

A handful of respondents were willing to answer questions but declined to suggest a team; their remarks are contained in a separate chapter. A couple of others agreed to contribute only if they were paid for it. The authors thought this unnecessary.

—N.A.
D.D.

Note on the Lineups

Most of our respondents did not specify outfield positions, opting instead simply to select three outfielders. The placement of outfielders in the graphics accompanying each lineup do not necessarily reflect either history or the intentions of the person who filled out the lineup.

Hall of Famer Teams

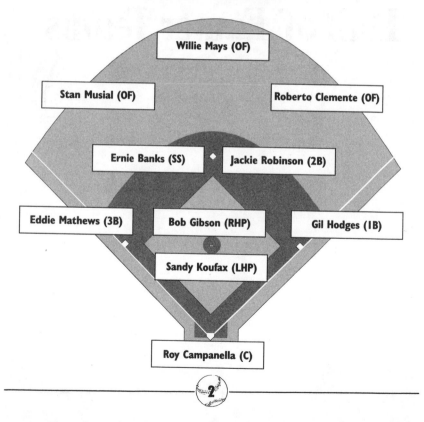

THE ULTIMATE LINEUP ACCORDING TO

Hank Aaron

Willie Mays (OF)

Stan Musial (OF)

Roberto Clemente (OF)

Ernie Banks (SS)

Jackie Robinson (2B)

Eddie Mathews (3B)

Bob Gibson (RHP)

Gil Hodges (1B)

Sandy Koufax (LHP)

Roy Campanella (C)

AARON HAS MORE home runs, runs batted in, and total bases than anyone else in the history of baseball. He is also third on the all-time list in games played, tied for second in runs scored, and third in hits. It would fill a volume to recap the righthand-hitting outfielder's records with the Braves in Milwaukee (1954-65) and Atlanta (1966-74), and again in Milwaukee with the Brewers (1975-76), but highlights of his remarkable career include 18 consecutive seasons with at least 20 home runs, 14 seasons batting over .300, 11 seasons with 100 or more runs batted in, 15 seasons with at least 100 runs scored, and a Most Valuable Player Award in 1957.

Given his career, it is hardly surprising that Aaron contends that "there wasn't any pitcher I felt I could never get a hit off." Nevertheless, he concedes that Juan Marichal and Don Drysdale rivaled Gibson as mound problems. "Hard-throwing righthanders who brushed you back were always tough. Some people remember that I hit more home runs off Drysdale than any other player did, but there were plenty of other at bats when he got me."

His toughest call is for catcher. "When he was healthy, there was nobody better than Campanella as both a catcher and a hitter. But I played with Del Crandall a long time and he was a match for anybody defensively."

hank aaron
NEW ALL-TIME HOME RUN KING
OUTFIELD • ATLANTA BRAVES

Aaron contends that "there wasn't any pitcher I felt I could never get a hit off."

Career Highlights
3,771 hits
2,297 runs batted in
2,174 runs scored
755 home runs
6,856 total bases
Most Valuable Player Award: 1957
Hall of Fame: 1982

THE ULTIMATE LINEUP ACCORDING TO

Luis Aparicio

Mickey Mantle (OF)

Frank Robinson (OF)

Al Kaline (OF)

Tony Kubek (SS)

Bobby Richardson (2B)

Brooks Robinson (3B)

Jim Palmer (RHP)

Vic Power (1B)

Dave McNally (LHP)

Bill Freehan (C)

ARGUABLY THE GREATEST defensive short-stop in American League history, Aparicio leads all shortstops in games played, career assists, and double plays. He batted .262 in 18 years with the White Sox (1956-62), Orioles (1963-67), White Sox again (1968-70), and Red Sox (1971-73). In 1956, he was Rookie of The Year, then went on to lead the American League in stolen bases for eight straight seasons. His best offensive year was probably 1960, when he stole 51 bases, scored 86 runs, and drove in another 61 from the leadoff spot.

In Aparicio's view, not even Frank Robinson's election to the Hall of Fame has brought the outfielder the recognition he deserved. "The thing about Frank was that he could beat you a hundred different ways—some of which didn't show up in the box score. When he didn't hit, he'd make a great catch or steal a base or kick a ball out of an infielder's glove. He always had something in mind, and I don't know of anybody who ever played the game who was more of a force on the field."

In addition to the lineup he has assembled, Aparicio would make room for two stars of the Minnesota Twins. "Tony Oliva was a pure hitter in the way they talk about Ted Williams. Before his legs gave out on him, he was second to nobody with a bat in his hands. I also could have done without facing Camilo Pascual."

LUIS APARICIO
SHORTSTOP—CHICAGO WHITE SOX

"Camilo Pascual . . . was the best curveball pitcher I ever saw. Nobody could make you look more foolish when you were in the batter's box."

Career Highlights
1,553 double plays
8,016 carrer assists
2,581 games played
Rookie of the Year: 1956
Hall of Fame: 1984

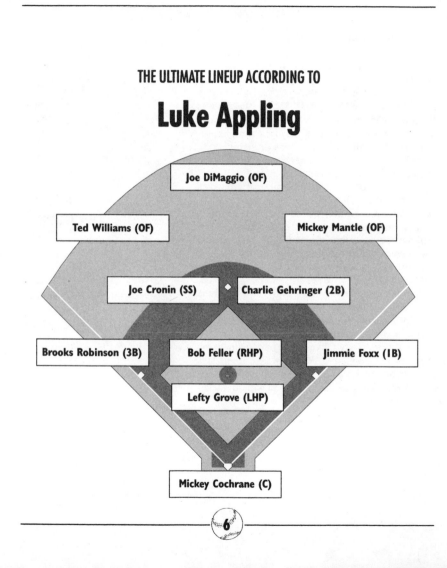

THE ULTIMATE LINEUP ACCORDING TO

Luke Appling

Joe DiMaggio (OF)

Ted Williams (OF)

Mickey Mantle (OF)

Joe Cronin (SS)

Charlie Gehringer (2B)

Brooks Robinson (3B)

Bob Feller (RHP)

Jimmie Foxx (1B)

Lefty Grove (LHP)

Mickey Cochrane (C)

THE RIGHTHAND-HITTING Appling batted .310 in twenty seasons (1930-43, 1945-50) with the White Sox. A lead-off hitter with the ability to foul off pitch after pitch, he won two batting championships, with averages of .388 in 1936 and .328 in 1943—the former the highest compiled by any twentieth-century shortstop. He batted over .300 in every season between 1933 and 1949, his last season as a regular (when he was 42).

The only non-contemporary Appling selected to his lineup is Mantle, who came along a year after the shortstop's retirement, and his only second thought was the possible substitution of Bill Dickey for Cochrane behind the plate.

According to Appling, "A team like this requires no comment. There's a reason why they're all in the Hall of Fame. The thing about playing against players of their calibre was that they eventually made you better. With the great pitchers, for instance, some days you can hit them, some days you can't, but if you're awake up there, you can learn something even when you're not successful in a given game. I ended up having some hits off Lefty Grove, but when I first came up, he just blew the ball by me. If you have any ability at all, it's all a learning process."

OLD ACHES AND PAINS
CHICAGO WHITE SOX – SHORTSTOP   1935

"With the great pitchers, some days you can hit them, some days you can't but if you're awake up there, you can learn something even when you're not successful in a given game."

Career Highlights
Lifetime batting average: .310
2 Batting Crowns
Hall of Fame: 1964

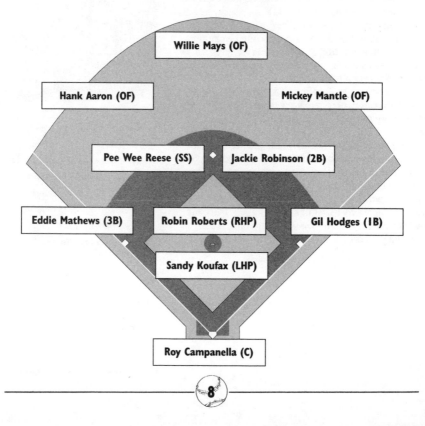

THE ULTIMATE LINEUP ACCORDING TO
Ernie Banks

Willie Mays (OF)

Hank Aaron (OF)

Mickey Mantle (OF)

Pee Wee Reese (SS)

Jackie Robinson (2B)

Eddie Mathews (3B)

Robin Roberts (RHP)

Gil Hodges (1B)

Sandy Koufax (LHP)

Roy Campanella (C)

BANKS SPENT HIS ENTIRE 19-year career (1953-71) with the Chicago Cubs, finishing with a .274 average and 512 home runs. The righthand-hitting slugger, who divided his work between shortstop and first base, led the National League in home runs and runs batted in twice, belted at least 40 homers five times, and drove in more than 100 runs eight times—almost always for clubs closer to the cellar than to first place. His best years were 1958, with a .313 average, 47 home runs, 23 doubles, 11 triples, 129 runs batted in, and 119 runs scored, and 1959 with a .304 average, 45 home runs, and 143 runs batted in—a fact acknowledged by sportswriters when he won back-to-back Most Valuable Player awards.

Banks was known for his gung-ho cry of "Let's play two!" Mr. Cub admits that even he was less than enthusiastic about getting into the box against Koufax or junkballer Stu Miller. "Koufax had everything—the pitches and the smarts to go with them. One of our hitters said once that what made Stu Miller aggravating was that you'd take this big swing and still see the ball over your back shoulder as you were completing your arc. I know what he meant. The ball *never* got there!"

Banks recalled what it was like to face junkballer Stu Miller at the plate. "Miller would drive me crazy with that junk he threw. Every time you'd think you had him timed, you'd still be out front."

Career Highlights
512 home runs
Most Valuable Player: 1958, 1959
Hall of Fame: 1977

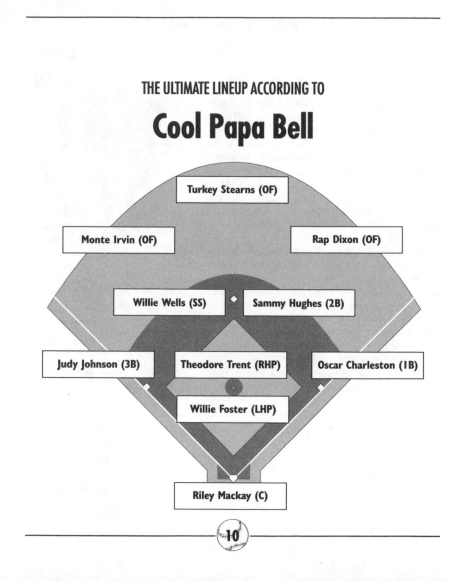

THE ULTIMATE LINEUP ACCORDING TO

Cool Papa Bell

Turkey Stearns (OF)

Monte Irvin (OF)

Rap Dixon (OF)

Willie Wells (SS)

Sammy Hughes (2B)

Judy Johnson (3B)

Theodore Trent (RHP)

Oscar Charleston (1B)

Willie Foster (LHP)

Riley Mackay (C)

A FLEET, SWITCH-HITTING center fielder, Bell had a lengthy career in the Negro Leagues and Latin America that began in 1922 and ran an incredible 29 years. He starred for such black teams as the St. Louis Stars, Detroit Wolves, Kansas City Monarchs, Pittsburgh Crawfords, Chicago American Giants, Memphis Red Sox, Homestead Grays, and Detroit Senators.

In 1937, he played in the Dominican Republic and spent five seasons in the Mexican League, where he hit a remarkable .437 in 1940 and led the league in just about every offensive category. He finally retired in 1950 after having played 29 summers in the United States and Latin America and 21 winters in Cuba and Puerto Rico. The following year, St. Louis Browns owner Bill Veeck sought to bring the veteran player into the American League, but Bell refused the offer. The approximate records compiled in the Negro Leagues indicate that he batted somewhere between .340 and .350.

In developing his lineup, Bell gave particular emphasis to his choices of outfielder Turkey Stearns and pitcher Theodore Trent. "Stearns, who played center for the Detroit Wolves, was flat out the greatest ballplayer I ever saw. He did everything, and better than everybody else. Trent died young of tuberculosis, but there was a stretch of about six years when no white all-star team could touch him."

Toughest pitcher? "All pitchers are tough when your timing is off. In general, though, I always preferred facing the older men. They knew what they were doing. Younger pitchers are just too wild."

Bell is the source of the joke about the baseball player who was so fast he could turn out the lights and be in bed before the room was dark.

Career Highlights
.340 to .350 batting average
Hall of Fame: 1974

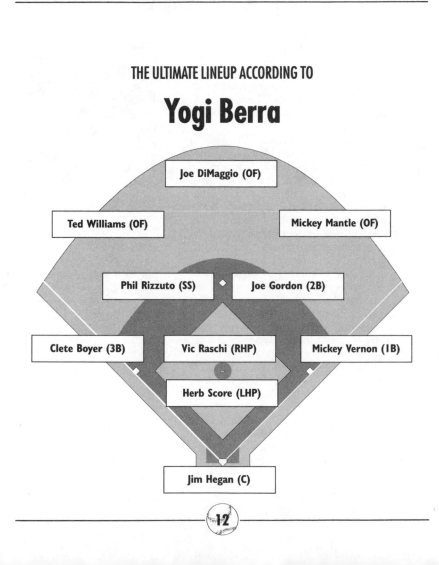

THE ULTIMATE LINEUP ACCORDING TO

Yogi Berra

Joe DiMaggio (OF)

Ted Williams (OF)

Mickey Mantle (OF)

Phil Rizzuto (SS)

Joe Gordon (2B)

Clete Boyer (3B)

Vic Raschi (RHP)

Mickey Vernon (1B)

Herb Score (LHP)

Jim Hegan (C)

ONE OF THE MOST POPULAR figures in baseball history, Berra batted .285 with 358 home runs and 1,430 runs batted in during his 18-year career with the New York Yankees (1946-63). The lefty-hitting catcher hit at least 20 home runs 11 times and drove in more than 100 runs in five seasons. Especially in his later years, Berra was known as baseball's best late-inning clutch hitter. His single best seasons were 1950 (.322, 28 home runs, 30 doubles, 124 runs batted in, 116 runs scored), and his American League Most Valuable Player seasons of 1951 (.294, 27 home runs, 88 RBIs), 1954 (.307, 22, 125), and 1955 (.272, 27, 108). He also holds a number of defensive records for his position. Berra, who had a handful of at bats for the Mets in 1965 to exploit his popularity in New York, also managed both his teams to pennants. He steered the Yankees to a flag in 1964, and did the same for the Mets in 1973.

Berra contends that his toughest mound opponent was Alex Kellner, a southpaw for the Philadelphia Athletics who had one 20-win season but finished with a career mark of 101-112 and led the American League in losses twice. "For a while there, he was far better than the team around him, and he could give me fits."

He chooses two teammates—Phil Rizzuto and Roger Maris—as the most underrated players of his era. "It's unbelievable that Phil had to wait so long to get to the Hall of Fame. Maris's home run record in 1961 has become something of a curse. He wasn't just a home run hitter, he could do everything—hit in the clutch, field, throw, and run."

Berra chooses two teammates—Phil Rizzuto and Roger Maris—as the most underrated players of his era.

Career Highlights
358 home runs
1,430 runs batted in
Most Valuable Player: 1951, 1954, 1955
Hall of Fame: 1971

THE ULTIMATE LINEUP ACCORDING TO
Lou Boudreau

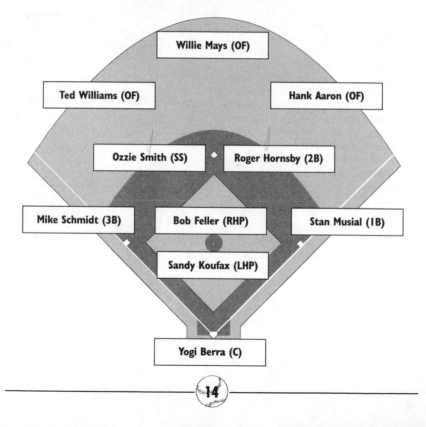

Willie Mays (OF)

Ted Williams (OF)

Hank Aaron (OF)

Ozzie Smith (SS)

Roger Hornsby (2B)

Mike Schmidt (3B)

Bob Feller (RHP)

Stan Musial (1B)

Sandy Koufax (LHP)

Yogi Berra (C)

IN 1942, AT AGE 24, Boudreau became the youngest manager to start a season. As a playing manager, the righthand-hitting shortstop batted .295 for the Indians (1938–1950) and Red Sox (1951–1952).

Boudreau clinched the American League batting title in 1944 with a .327 average, and he paced the circuit with the most doubles three times. His best season was 1948 when, in a one-game playoff against the Red Sox that decided the league's pennant, he went four-for-four with two home runs and steered the Indians to a world championship. That same year brought him the Most Valuable Player award for his .355 average, 18 home runs, 106 runs batted in, and 116 runs scored. He later managed the Red Sox, Athletics, and Cubs.

In choosing his lineup, Boudreau included Sandy Koufax, yet acknowledges that he never had to face him. "But seeing him as a manager and broadcaster was about as close as I wanted to get to him." His own toughest pitchers were "from the left side Hal Newhouser and from the right side Red Ruffing. They weren't very similar, but I found it hard to pick up their pitches."

In Boudreau's opinion that the most underrated player of his time was Ken Keltner. "He was never the kind of flashy third baseman who would attract the media, but was a great gloveman and could hit the long ball."

Career Highlights
Batting Crown: 1944
Most Valuable Player: 1948
Hall of Fame: 1970

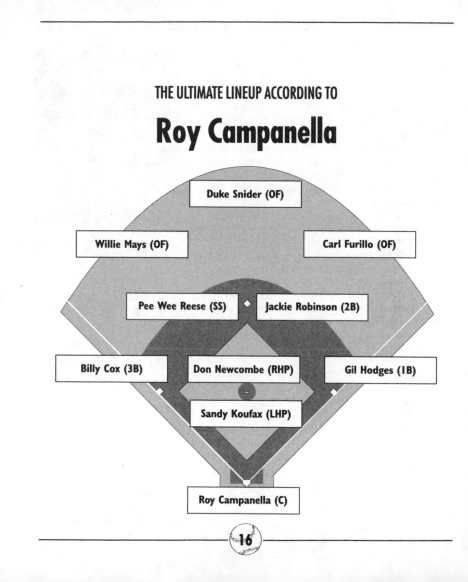

THE ULTIMATE LINEUP ACCORDING TO

Roy Campanella

Duke Snider (OF)

Willie Mays (OF)

Carl Furillo (OF)

Pee Wee Reese (SS)

Jackie Robinson (2B)

Billy Cox (3B)

Don Newcombe (RHP)

Gil Hodges (1B)

Sandy Koufax (LHP)

Roy Campanella (C)

CAMPANELLA WENT FROM a brief but outstanding career in the Negro Leagues to the Brooklyn Dodgers, where he was the regular catcher on the Boys of Summer teams from 1948 to 1957. Hampered by injuries for most of his career, he still managed to clout 242 home runs and bat .276 lifetime. While playing with the Dodgers, the righthand-hitting slugger won the National League Most Valuable Player award in three seasons—1951 when he hit .325 with 33 home runs, 33 doubles, and 108 runs batted in; 1953 when he batted .312 with 41 homers, 103 runs scored, and a league-leading 142 runs batted in; and 1955 when he hit .318 with 32 home runs and 107 runs scored. His career came to an end when an automobile accident left him confined to a wheelchair for life.

Campanella saw no reason to apologize for all the teammates (everyone but Mays) in his lineup. "Do you have to ask? Willie was pretty good, and we never really had a regular left fielder all those years, so I guess I can make room for him in there somewhere."

"In the Negro Leagues my toughest pitcher had to be Satchel Paige, who threw hard and had outstanding control. For the National League, I'd have to mention three righthanders. Ewell Blackwell because his ball moved *so* much; the man was incapable of throwing anything straight, almost like a lefthander. Robin Roberts because he had excellent control and always knew how to hit the spots. And Sal Maglie because he had a tremendous curve that he could throw at different speeds."

Campanella set new standards for catchers defensively.

Career Highlights
242 home runs
Most Valuable Player: 1951, 1953, 1955
Hall of Fame: 1969

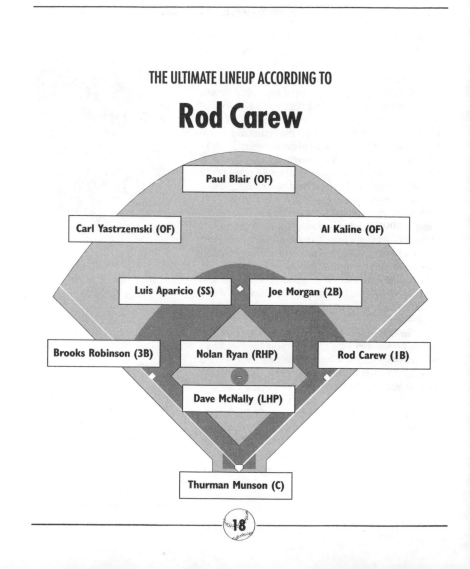

THE ULTIMATE LINEUP ACCORDING TO

Rod Carew

Paul Blair (OF)

Carl Yastrzemski (OF)

Al Kaline (OF)

Luis Aparicio (SS)

Joe Morgan (2B)

Brooks Robinson (3B)

Nolan Ryan (RHP)

Rod Carew (1B)

Dave McNally (LHP)

Thurman Munson (C)

CAREW BATTED .338 and won seven American League batting crowns during his 19 seasons with the Twins (1967-78) and Angels (1979-1985). He won four of those crowns consecutively from 1972 to 1975.

A second baseman who switched to first base midway through his career, the lefty batter collected 3,053 hits, finished four seasons with 200 or more hits, and led the league in hits three times. In 1969, he stole home seven times, out of a career total of 19. His best year was 1977 when he hit .388 and led the American League in hits with 239 (the highest total in the major leagues since 1930), in triples with 16, and in runs scored with 128.

In choosing his lineup, Carew contends that McNally "just beats out Mike Cuellar. It was never any fun playing Baltimore when they had those two coming at you one after the other."

"Most of this team is designed for offense, though some of the hitters—like Brooks Robinson and Thurman Munson—were as good as you could get at their positions. At shortstop you have to have Luis Aparicio. No one covered more ground or had better hands. And in center you'd need someone who could go get the ball better than anyone else, and that would be Blair. As for first base, well, if I have to win one game, I want to be there."

Carew admits that the toughest pitcher he faced was Rudy May. "And to be honest about it I don't know why. He just got me out. All I know is that I was glad to see him go to the National League for a few years."

Career Highlights
3,053 hits
Rookie of the Year: 1967
Most Valuable Player: 1977
7 Batting Crowns
Hall of Fame: 1991

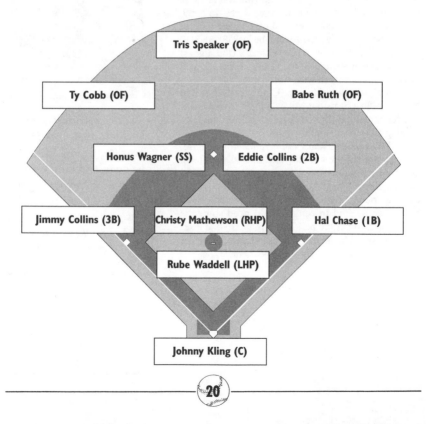

THE ULTIMATE LINEUP ACCORDING TO

Fred Clarke

Tris Speaker (OF)

Ty Cobb (OF)

Babe Ruth (OF)

Honus Wagner (SS)

Eddie Collins (2B)

Jimmy Collins (3B)

Christy Mathewson (RHP)

Hal Chase (1B)

Rube Waddell (LHP)

Johnny Kling (C)

CLARKE, A LEFTY-HITTING OUTFIELDER, batted .315 over 21 seasons with the Louisville Colonels (1894-99) and the Pittsburgh Pirates (1900-15). In his first major league game he went five-for-five, a debut matched only once. A player-manager from 1897 until the end of his career, the feisty Clarke hit .390 in 1897 and in one season or another led the National League in doubles, triples, walks, and slugging percentage. As manager of the Pirates, he won 945 games between 1901 and 1910, and won three consecutive pennants between 1901 and 1903 and a world championship in 1909.

Wagner and Waddell are the members of his lineup he played with or managed, and only Christy Mathewson, Hal Chase, and Johnny Kling were fellow National Leaguers. The only non-Hall of Famers Clarke selected are first baseman Chase—who was blacklisted after a long series of charges that he had thrown games—and catcher Kling, a .271 hitter over 13 years. A member of the Tinker-to-Evers-to-Chance Cubs at the beginning of the century, Kling was renowned as a defensive specialist who helped guide Three Finger Brown, among others, to success.

F. CLARKE, PITTSBURG

Clarke was one of the most successful player-managers in baseball history.

Career Highlights
Lifetime batting average: .315
Hall of Fame: 1945

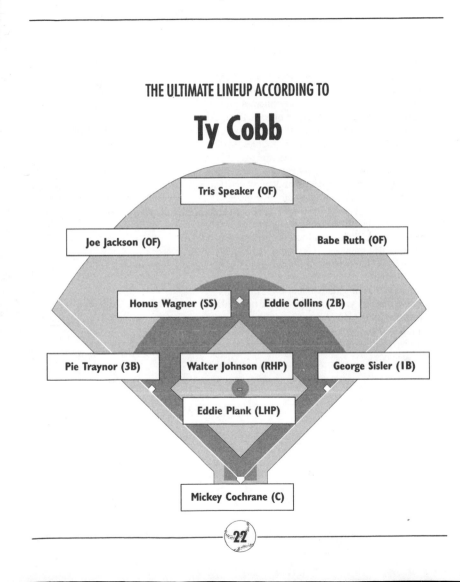

THE ULTIMATE LINEUP ACCORDING TO

Ty Cobb

Tris Speaker (OF)

Joe Jackson (OF)

Babe Ruth (OF)

Honus Wagner (SS)

Eddie Collins (2B)

Pie Traynor (3B)

Walter Johnson (RHP)

George Sisler (1B)

Eddie Plank (LHP)

Mickey Cochrane (C)

RIVALED ONLY BY BABE RUTH as the best player in baseball history, Cobb hit a record .367 during his 24-year career with the Tigers (1905-26) and the Athletics (1927-28). Along the way he captured 12 batting titles, as well as a reputation as one of the meanest, most aggressive players ever to don a uniform. The lefty-hitting outfielder also led the American League in home runs once, doubles three times, triples and runs batted in four times , runs scored five times, stolen bases six times, and hits eight times. His 892 lifetime stolen bases and 4,191 career hits stood as records until 1978 and 1985, respectively.

Cobb, who made his selections five years before his death in 1961, chose all contemporaries to his lineup. Alternatives he suggested were Bill Dickey behind the plate, Christy Mathewson and Grover Cleveland Alexander as righthanded pitchers, and Lefty Grove as the southpaw.

Cobb often said that the pitcher who gave him the most grief was Carl Weilman, a lefthander who had an 84-94 record and a 2.67 ERA with the Browns in eight seasons (1912-17, 1919-20.)

COBB, DETROIT

Not only did Cobb bat over .300 23 times, but he topped .400 in three seasons.

Career Highlights

.367 lifetime batting average

4,191 hits

2,245 runs scored

12 Batting Crowns

Hall of Fame: 1936

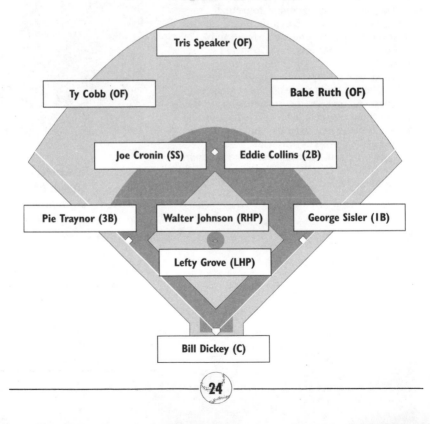

THE ULTIMATE LINEUP ACCORDING TO
Mickey Cochrane

Tris Speaker (OF)

Ty Cobb (OF)

Babe Ruth (OF)

Joe Cronin (SS)

Eddie Collins (2B)

Pie Traynor (3B)

Walter Johnson (RHP)

George Sisler (1B)

Lefty Grove (LHP)

Bill Dickey (C)

COCHRANE'S CAREER MARK of .320 in 13 seasons with the Athletics (1925-33) and the Tigers (1934-37) stands as the record for big-league catchers. His best years were with the pennant-winning A's between 1929 and 1931, when he batted .331, .357, and .349.

A noted contact hitter who never struck out more than 25 times in a season, he also banged out 119 home runs, reaching double figures six times. Cochrane scored more than 100 runs four times. With the Tigers, he served as a player-manager, piloting the team to pennants in both 1934 and 1935. His career was cut short when he was beaned by Yankee hurler Bump Hadley.

As Cochrane's lineup stands, Traynor is the lone National Leaguer. As an alternative to Dickey, Cochrane suggested Gabby Hartnett. In a written note, Cochrane explained his choice of Cronin at shortstop by saying only that he "didn't see Honus Wagner."

Cochrane posted a .400 batting average in the 1929 World Series.

Career Highlights
Lifetime batting average: .320
119 home runs
Most Valuable Player: 1928
Hall of Fame: 1947

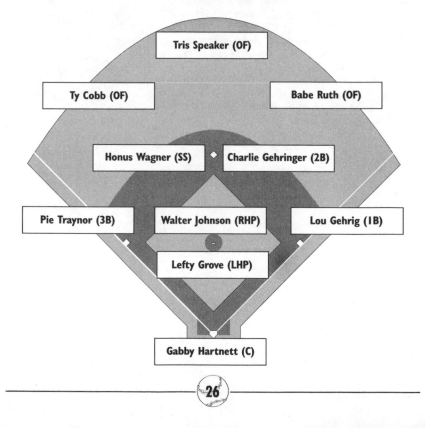

THE ULTIMATE LINEUP ACCORDING TO
Jocko Conlan

Tris Speaker (OF)

Ty Cobb (OF)

Babe Ruth (OF)

Honus Wagner (SS)

Charlie Gehringer (2B)

Pie Traynor (3B)

Walter Johnson (RHP)

Lou Gehrig (1B)

Lefty Grove (LHP)

Gabby Hartnett (C)

THE FOURTH UMPIRE ELECTED to the Hall of Fame, Conlan went into umpiring after a couple of seasons as an outfielder for the White Sox (1934-35), for whom he batted .263 with little power. He joined the National League umpiring staff in 1941 and went on to officiate in six World Series, six All-Star games, and four National League playoffs. His tussles with Leo Durocher were a regular feature of 1950s baseball.

Conlan had a lot more to say about the people not in his lineup than those who made it. "Bill Terry was the next best thing to Gehrig, but no one was more graceful at first base than Hal Chase. He could throw guys out at third on a bunt. But I don't want him on my team because he was a crook. Buck Weaver, on the other hand, wasn't a crook, though some people have the impression that he was. Commissioner Landis threw him out of baseball because he knew about the plot to throw the 1919 World Series, not because he himself threw any games.

"Joe Dugan, who was a pretty good third baseman with the Yankees, once told me, 'We all learned to play third base watching Weaver.' I think that says how good he was.

"There are only two men in baseball I didn't like—Durocher and Jackie Robinson. Both of them always used bad language. Durocher knew the game, but he couldn't handle men. I would say that George Stallings was the best manager I ever saw. Anybody can manage all-stars or future Hall of Famers, but Stallings worked with guys who were really so-so and still made them winners."

Conlan also noted a similarity in the two pitchers he chose. "Neither Johnson nor Grove had a curve ball. But they never had sore arms, either."

"I would say that George Stallings was the best manager I ever saw."

Career Highlights
Hall of Fame: 1974

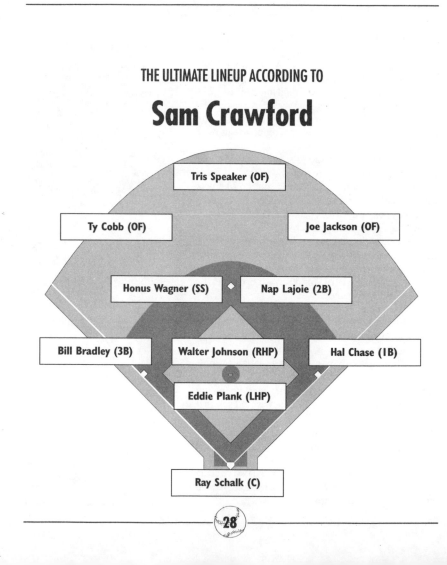

THE ULTIMATE LINEUP ACCORDING TO

Sam Crawford

Tris Speaker (OF)

Ty Cobb (OF)

Joe Jackson (OF)

Honus Wagner (SS)

Nap Lajoie (2B)

Bill Bradley (3B)

Walter Johnson (RHP)

Hal Chase (1B)

Eddie Plank (LHP)

Ray Schalk (C)

AS NOTED for his speed and defense as for his offense, Crawford batted .309 in a 19-year career with the Reds (1899-1902) and Tigers (1903-17). The lefthand-batting outfielder was particularly proficient at three-base hits; he led the National League once and the American League five times in triples, and his 312 three-baggers make him the all-time leader in that category. He is also one of the rare major leaguers to lead both circuits in home runs. Before retiring, Crawford also led the American League in doubles once, in runs scored once, and in runs batted in three times.

Crawford's choice of Joe Jackson as one of his outfielders mirrors the opinion of most early-century players that "Shoeless Joe" was one of the greatest hitters of the game. Before being ostracized for his involvement in the Black Sox scandal in the 1919 World Series, Jackson had a career average of .356. To cover third base, Crawford chose Bill Bradley, an outstanding defensive baseman who hit .271 in his 14-year career spent mostly with Cleveland (1901-10). Crawford gave home plate to Ray Schalk, who, despite his Cooperstown plaque, is not usually considered among the game's great receivers.

Crawford is one of the rare major leaguers to lead both leagues in home runs.

Career Highlights
312 triples
Hall of Fame: 1957

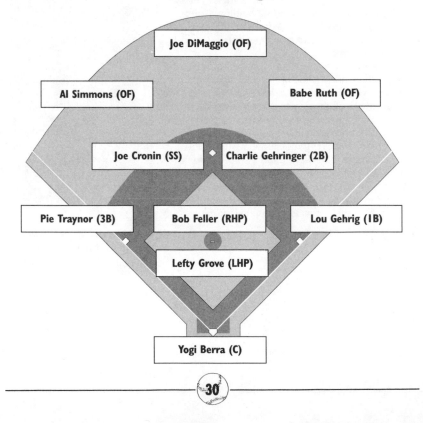

THE ULTIMATE LINEUP ACCORDING TO

Bill Dickey

Joe DiMaggio (OF)

Al Simmons (OF)

Babe Ruth (OF)

Joe Cronin (SS)

Charlie Gehringer (2B)

Pie Traynor (3B)

Bob Feller (RHP)

Lou Gehrig (1B)

Lefty Grove (LHP)

Yogi Berra (C)

THE LEFTY-SWINGING DICKEY batted .313 in a 17-year career spent exclusively with the Yankees (1928-43, 1946). His .362 average in 1936 marks the season high for an American League catcher. No banjo hitter, Dickey hit 202 home runs and had four straight years (1936-39) with at least 22 homers and 105 runs batted in. His defensive skills have also contributed to his reputation as arguably the best catcher in American League history.

Dickey's selections to his lineup were all contemporaries and, with the exception of Pie Traynor, all fellow American Leaguers.

For Dickey, the toughest pitcher he ever faced was also the most underrated player of his era. "Hands down, Johnny Allen. He had good control and could come completely sidearm or straight overhand. When he was with the Yankees, he was awfully hard to catch. When he went to other teams, I found him just as hard to hit." Allen pitched for five teams in 13 seasons (1933-44), winning 142 and losing 75 with a 3.75 ERA.

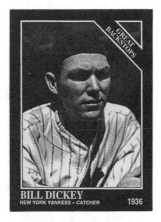

BILL DICKEY
NEW YORK YANKEES – CATCHER   1936

With the Yankees, Dickey appeared in seven World Series between 1936 and 1943. The Bronx Bombers won six times.

Career Highlights
202 home runs
Lifetime batting average: .313
Hall of Fame: 1954

31

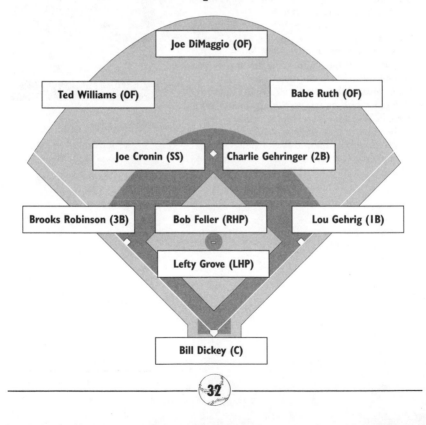

THE ULTIMATE LINEUP ACCORDING TO

Bobby Doerr

Joe DiMaggio (OF)

Ted Williams (OF)

Babe Ruth (OF)

Joe Cronin (SS)

Charlie Gehringer (2B)

Brooks Robinson (3B)

Bob Feller (RHP)

Lou Gehrig (1B)

Lefty Grove (LHP)

Bill Dickey (C)

DOERR PLAYED MORE GAMES exclusively at second base than anyone else, and he played them all for the Red Sox (1937-44, 1946-51). A sterling defensive player and a righthanded hitter with clout, he batted .288 with 223 home runs. He averaged over .300 three times, belted at least 15 homers in 10 consecutive seasons, and drove home more than 100 runs six times.

Doerr's best year was 1944, when he hit .325 and led the American League in slugging. In his only World Series, in 1946, Doerr hit .409.

Doerr wonders why anyone *wouldn't* pick Bob Feller as the toughest pitcher. "For a long time, he had the best fastball to go along with one of the great curves. He was totally dominating."

His most underrated contemporary was "Ken Keltner of Cleveland. He wasn't very spectacular, but he was always steady and he had an accurate arm. At bat he always seemed to save his best for clutch situations."

BOBBY DOERR
A SCOUT'S DREAM
1940

According to Doerr, his most underrated contemporary was Ken Ketlner.

Career Highlights
223 home runs
Hall of Fame: 1986

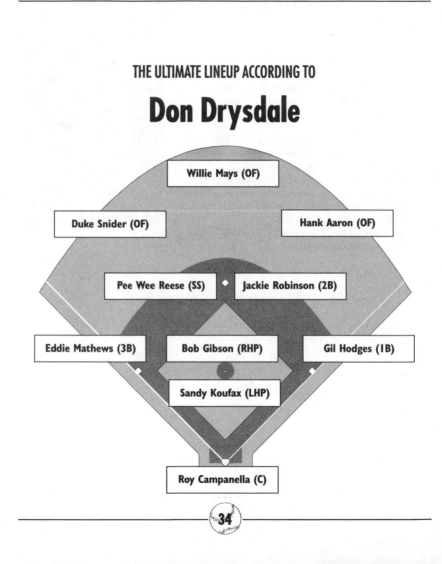

THE ULTIMATE LINEUP ACCORDING TO

Don Drysdale

Willie Mays (OF)

Duke Snider (OF)

Hank Aaron (OF)

Pee Wee Reese (SS)

Jackie Robinson (2B)

Eddie Mathews (3B)

Bob Gibson (RHP)

Gil Hodges (1B)

Sandy Koufax (LHP)

Roy Campanella (C)

DRYSDALE TEAMED UP WITH southpaw Sandy Koufax in the 1960s to give Los Angeles one of the most potent righty-lefty pitching tandems in the history of the game. A Dodger from 1956 to 1969, he won 209 games against 166 losses, struck out 2,486 batters, and wound up with a 2.93 ERA. He won more than 20 games a season twice, led the league in strikeouts three times, and once hurled 58 consecutive scoreless innings (a record later broken by another Los Angeles righthander, Orel Hershiser).

Drysdale's best year was 1962, when he took the Cy Young Award for a league-leading 25 victories and 2.83 ERA. No slouch as a hitter, he had 29 career home runs, seven of them in 1965 alone.

"Let's just say there were too many tough batters to mention one. Even guys I got out regularly became the toughest when they came to bat with the winning run on base."

As for the most underrated player, "I suppose I'm betraying my Brooklyn beginnings with the Dodgers, but I'd say Carl Furillo. A lot of the others got more publicity, but in the field and at bat he was their equal in most ways."

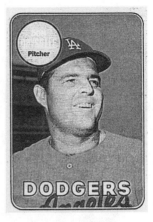

Drysdale and teammate Sandy Koufax were the most imposing starting duo in the National League in the early- and mid-1960s.

Career Highlights
209 wins
Cy Young Award: 1962
Hall of Fame: 1984

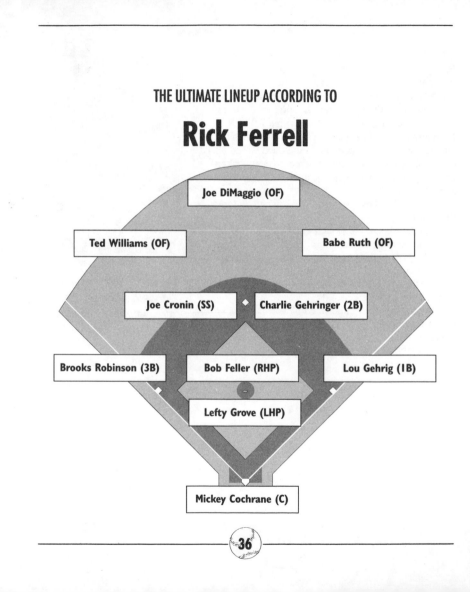

THE ULTIMATE LINEUP ACCORDING TO

Rick Ferrell

Joe DiMaggio (OF)

Ted Williams (OF)

Babe Ruth (OF)

Joe Cronin (SS)

Charlie Gehringer (2B)

Brooks Robinson (3B)

Bob Feller (RHP)

Lou Gehrig (1B)

Lefty Grove (LHP)

Mickey Cochrane (C)

FERRELL, WHO HAD CAUGHT more American League games than any other receiver until Carlton Fisk came along, spent most of his 18-year career with second-division clubs, which cost him the attention he deserved for his sparkling defense and .281 batting average. The righthanded batsman played for the Browns (1929-33, 1941-43), Red Sox (1933-37), and Senators (1937-41, 1944-45, 1947) when the three teams could call .500 a banner year. Ferrell's best years were for the Browns in 1931 and 1932, with averages of .306 and .315, respectively, and for the Red Sox in 1935 and 1936, with a .301 and .312 respectively.

In his lineup, Ferrell includes a non-contemporary, third baseman Brooks Robinson. "He wasn't in my era, but he would have been my pick there for any era. Nobody ever played third like he did."

"The most underrated player would have to be Jimmie Foxx. He's in the Hall of Fame, but I never thought he got his due. Look at my own lineup. Even I left him out behind those others."

With Boston and Washington between 1934 and 1938, Ferrell formed an all-star sibling battery with his brother, Wes.

Career Highlights
1,805 games caught
Hall of Fame: 1984

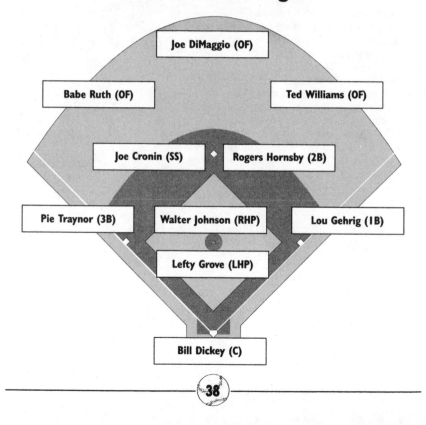

THE ULTIMATE LINEUP ACCORDING TO

Charlie Gehringer

Joe DiMaggio (OF)

Babe Ruth (OF)

Ted Williams (OF)

Joe Cronin (SS)

Rogers Hornsby (2B)

Pie Traynor (3B)

Walter Johnson (RHP)

Lou Gehrig (1B)

Lefty Grove (LHP)

Bill Dickey (C)

GEHRINGER SPENT his entire career with the Tigers (1924-42). Batting .320, he was dubbed "Mechanical Man" for his ability to stroke base hits automatically. For 14 of his 19 big league seasons, the lefty swinger batted over .300; he captured the hitting title and the American League Most Valuable Player Award in 1937 for his .371 average. Gehringer also led the American league in doubles twice, triples once, runs scored twice, hits twice, and stolen bases once. He collected a minimum of 200 hits seven times, of 100 runs scored twelve times, and of 100 runs batted in on seven occasions.

Gehringer selected his team when asked initially in the 1950s. Reinterviewed more than 30 years later, he insisted that the changes constantly assailing baseball made it impossible to pick a single all-time, all-star team. "Maybe every ten years you can pick one because the players would have been playing under similar conditions. But at least for me, it's impossible to sort out players after witnessing baseball for more than 60 years. There've just been too many drastic changes — speeded-up balls, big gloves, Astroturf, expanded leagues, the effect of high salaries, just to name a few. Let's just say that the team I picked originally covers from the 1920s to the late 1940s."

THE MECHANICAL MAN
DETROIT TIGERS – 2ND BASE   1934

Although not regarded as a power hitter, Gehringer got into double figures in the home run category eleven times.

Career Highlights
Most Valuable Player: 1937
Lifetime batting average: .320
Hall of Fame: 1949

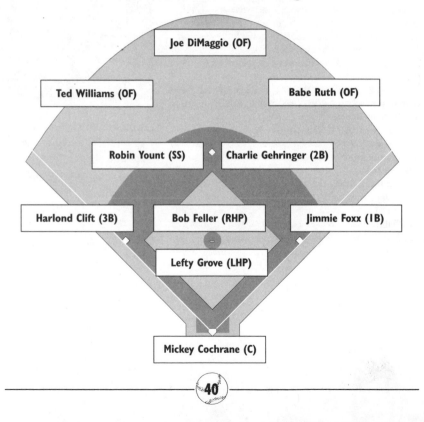

THE ULTIMATE LINEUP ACCORDING TO

Hank Greenberg

Joe DiMaggio (OF)

Ted Williams (OF)

Babe Ruth (OF)

Robin Yount (SS)

Charlie Gehringer (2B)

Harlond Clift (3B)

Bob Feller (RHP)

Jimmie Foxx (IB)

Lefty Grove (LHP)

Mickey Cochrane (C)

GREENBERG SPENT 12 of his 13 major league seasons with the Tigers (1930, 1933-41, 1945-47) as one of the foremost sluggers in the American League. The righty-swinging first baseman-outfielder amassed 331 home runs and 1,276 runs batted in to go with a lifetime .313 average—numbers affected seriously by his lengthy military service during World War II.

His career highlights include walloping 58 home runs in 1938; driving home 183 runs in 1937; leading the American League in homers four times, in runs batted in four times, and in doubles twice; scoring more than 100 runs six times and driving home more than 100 seven times; and taking Most Valuable Player awards in 1935 and 1940. He spent his final year with the Pirates, clouting 25 home runs off National League pitchers and helping to polish the skills of Ralph Kiner.

Greenberg's lineup includes some significant changes from a team he put together several decades earlier. In his original picks, he had Lou Gehrig at first instead of Foxx, Pie Traynor at third instead of Clift, Honus Wagner at short rather than Yount, and Ty Cobb in the outfield rather than Williams. The reasons for the changes? "I never played against Cobb or Wagner or Traynor. Obviously I never played against Yount either, but I've seen a lot of him. And as for Foxx versus Gehrig, well, either way, how do you lose?"

Greenberg's lengthy service in the military during World War II prevented him from compiling even greater slugging records.

Career Highlights
331 home runs
1,276 runs batted in
Most Valuable Player: 1935, 1940
Hall of Fame: 1956

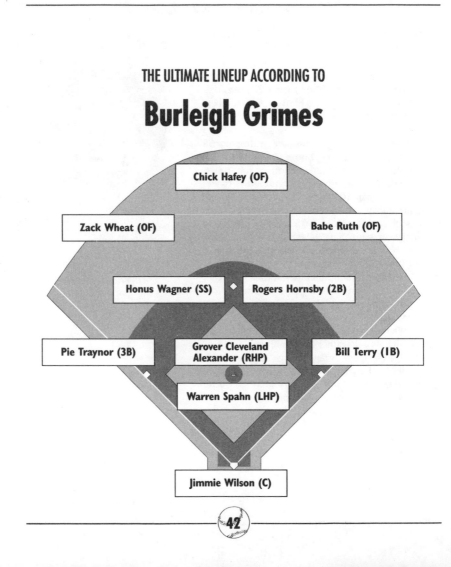

THE ULTIMATE LINEUP ACCORDING TO

Burleigh Grimes

Chick Hafey (OF)

Zack Wheat (OF)

Babe Ruth (OF)

Honus Wagner (SS)

Rogers Hornsby (2B)

Pie Traynor (3B)

Grover Cleveland Alexander (RHP)

Bill Terry (1B)

Warren Spahn (LHP)

Jimmie Wilson (C)

RIGHTHANDER GRIMES, THE LAST of the legal spitballers, compiled a 270-212 record in 19 years of major league service (1916-1934). One of Cooperstown's more conspicuous vagabonds, he entered the big leagues with the Pirates, then went on to the Dodgers, Giants, a second tour with the Pirates, Braves, Cardinals, Cubs, Cardinals again, Pirates for a third time, and, finally, the Yankees. His achievements include winning more than 20 games in five seasons and leading the league in complete games four times and in strikeouts once.

His single best season was probably for Pittsburgh in 1928, when he won 25 games and had an ERA of 2.99, but he didn't embarrass Brooklyn earlier in 1920 (23 wins, 2.33) or 1921 (22 wins, 2.83). Known for his rubber arm, he pitched 4,179 2/3 innings with his various clubs. He was also a good hitter, collecting 42 safeties in 1928 and at least 30 in three other seasons.

The least known members of Grimes's lineup are Chick Hafey and Jimmie Wilson. Elected to the Hall of Fame in 1971, righty-swinging Hafey batted .317 in 13 years with the Cardinals and Reds. Perhaps the National League's best defensive catcher between Johnny Kling and Roy Campanella, Wilson had an 18-year career with the Phillies, Cardinals, and Reds, batting .284 and starring in the 1940 World Series for Cincinnati at the age of 40.

Grimes also proposed "an alternate team of George Sisler, Frankie Frisch, Freddie Lindstrom, Charley Gelbert, Paul Waner, Mel Ott, Ross Youngs, Gabby Hartnett, Dazzy Vance, and Rube Marquard."

HOF · 1964

BURLEIGH GRIMES
PITTSBURGH PIRATES – PITCHER 1928

The last legal spitballer, Grimes played on seven teams over his 19-year career.

Career Highlights
270 wins
Hall of Fame: 1964

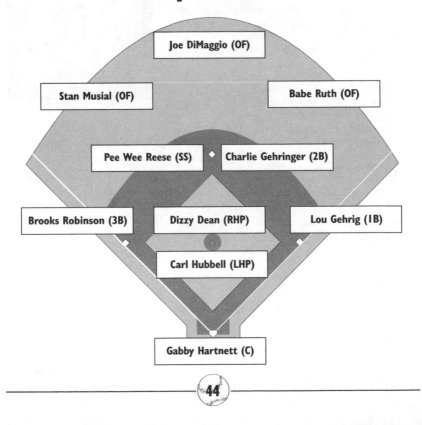

THE ULTIMATE LINEUP ACCORDING TO
Billy Herman

Joe DiMaggio (OF)

Stan Musial (OF)

Babe Ruth (OF)

Pee Wee Reese (SS)

Charlie Gehringer (2B)

Brooks Robinson (3B)

Dizzy Dean (RHP)

Lou Gehrig (1B)

Carl Hubbell (LHP)

Gabby Hartnett (C)

SECOND BASEMAN HERMAN batted .304 in 15 seasons with the Cubs (1931-41), Dodgers (1941-43, 1946), Braves (1946), and Pirates (1947). He topped the .300 mark in seven of the 13 seasons in which he played more than 100 games and scored more than 100 runs five times. Herman's best season was 1935 when he led the National League in hits and doubles and averaged .341 for the pennant-winning Cubs. He closed out his active career as a player-manager for the Pirates and later managed the Red Sox from 1964 to 1966.

Included in his lineup are Reese, Hartnett, and Dean, Herman's teammates at one time or another. The same trio, plus Musial and Hubbell, were opponents in various seasons. As for his other choices, "Gehrig, Ruth, and DiMaggio were Gehrig, Ruth, and DiMaggio. I saw enough of Gehringer to know that he was the full goods at second base. Why would I pick another National Leaguer instead of myself? As for Robinson, I saw enough of him when I was managing the Red Sox and coaching in the American League. There's never been any better."

*Herman was a lifetime
.304 hitter in 15 big
league seasons.*

Career Highlights
Lifetime batting average: .304
Hall of Fame: 1975

45

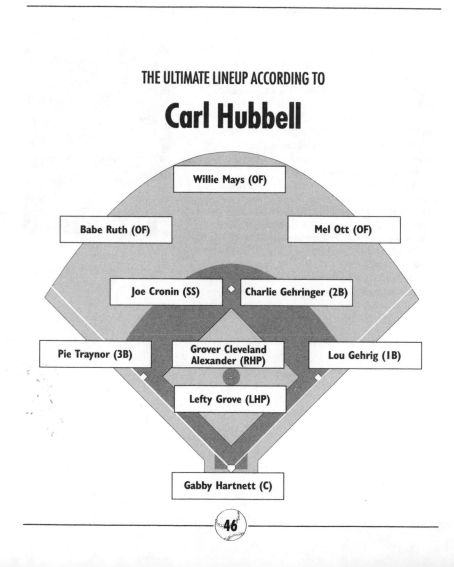

THE ULTIMATE LINEUP ACCORDING TO

Carl Hubbell

Willie Mays (OF)

Babe Ruth (OF)

Mel Ott (OF)

Joe Cronin (SS)

Charlie Gehringer (2B)

Pie Traynor (3B)

Grover Cleveland Alexander (RHP)

Lou Gehrig (1B)

Lefty Grove (LHP)

Gabby Hartnett (C)

SOUTHPAW HUBBELL SPENT his entire 16-year career with the Giants (1928-43), compiling a record of 253-154 with a 2.97 ERA. The screwballer led the National League in victories three times, in strikeouts once, and in shutouts once; he won Most Valuable Player awards in 1933 and 1936. In the latter season, he turned in a sparkling record of 26-6 with an ERA of 2.31, and began his record streak of 24 victories—his final 16 games of 1936 and his first eight of 1937. In six World Series appearances, he won 4 and lost 2, posting a 1.79 ERA.

Gehringer, Grove, Gehrig, Cronin, and Ruth were all American Leaguers, whom Hubbell faced only in World Series and All-Star games; the last three were among the five consecutive strikeouts he recorded in the 1934 All Star Game. The only selection not from Hubbell's time was Mays, but he had ample opportunity to see the Giants outfielder regularly as a longtime executive for both the New York and San Francisco versions of the franchise.

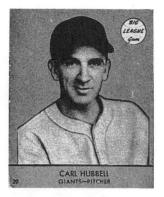

CARL HUBBELL
GIANTS—PITCHER

Hubbell's 16-year career with the Giants included four World Series appearances, two Most Valuable Player Awards, and a record streak of 24 wins.

Career Highlights
Lifetime record: 253-154
Lifetime ERA: 2.97
Posted five 20-win seasons
Most Valuable Player: 1933, 1936
Hall of Fame: 1947

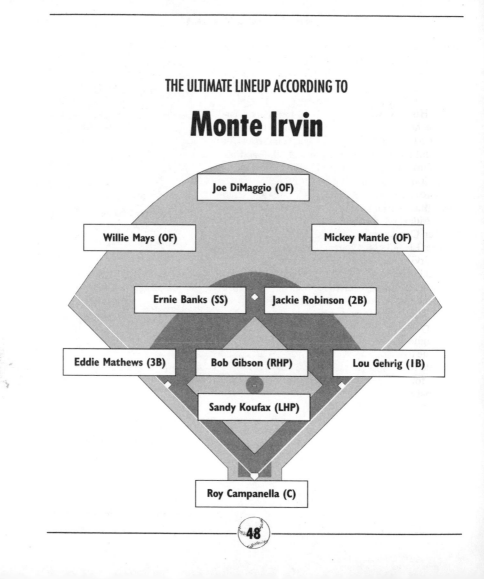

THE ULTIMATE LINEUP ACCORDING TO

Monte Irvin

Joe DiMaggio (OF)

Willie Mays (OF)

Mickey Mantle (OF)

Ernie Banks (SS)

Jackie Robinson (2B)

Eddie Mathews (3B)

Bob Gibson (RHP)

Lou Gehrig (1B)

Sandy Koufax (LHP)

Roy Campanella (C)

AFTER AN IMPRESSIVE CAREER with the Newark Eagles in the Negro Leagues, outfielder-first baseman Irvin played eight seasons in the National League—seven with the Giants (1949-55) and a final one with the Cubs (1956).

His best season in a .293 career was 1951, when he batted .312 with 24 home runs and a league-leading 121 runs batted in. That same year, he went 11-for-24 (.458) in the World Series against the Yankees.

Irvin's asterisk to his ideal major league lineup was to select one for the Negro Leagues as well: 1B–Buck Leonard; 2B–Sammy Hughes; 3B–Ray Dandridge; OF–Martin Dihigo, Cool Papa Bell, and Oscar Charleston; C–Josh Gibson; RHP–Satchel Paige; LHP–Willie Foster.

Irvin cited Ewell Blackwell as his toughest National League foe. "He was all legs and came whipping around at any righthanded hitter. I was always amazed that he didn't win more games than he did."

The most underrated players of his time were "Larry Doby and Richie Ashburn. Doby went through a lot of the same things in the American League that Robinson did in the National, and some people forget that he was the best power hitter over there for quite a few seasons. Ashburn was a great defensive center fielder and the perfect leadoff man."

MONTE IRVIN
outfielder NEW YORK GIANTS

According to Irvin, the most underrated players of his time were Larry Doby and Richie Ashburn.

Career Highlights
Posted .394 career World Series batting average
.400 hitter in Negro League
Hall of Fame: 1971

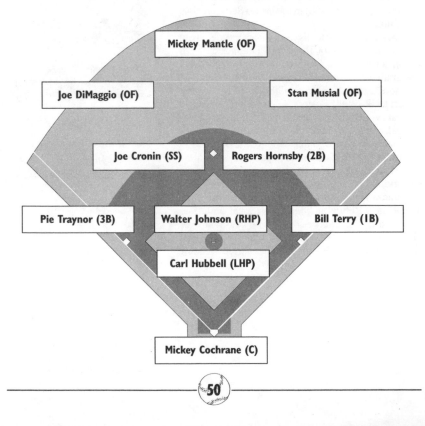

THE ULTIMATE LINEUP ACCORDING TO
Travis Jackson

Mickey Mantle (OF)

Joe DiMaggio (OF)

Stan Musial (OF)

Joe Cronin (SS)

Rogers Hornsby (2B)

Pie Traynor (3B)

Walter Johnson (RHP)

Bill Terry (1B)

Carl Hubbell (LHP)

Mickey Cochrane (C)

SHORTSTOP JACKSON WAS CONSIDERED one of the best gloves at his position. He batted .291 in the 15 seasons he spent with the Giants (1922-36). The right-handed hitter topped the .300 mark six times, with a career high of .339 in 1930. He reached double figures in home runs six times, hitting as many as 21 in 1929, probably his best season. That year, he batted .294, drove in 94 runs, and scored another 92. In 1934, he drove home 101 runs. Jackson's election to Cooperstown completed the only three all-Hall-of-Fame infields. Of course, they were all Giants. In 1925, first baseman Bill Terry, second baseman George Kelly, and third baseman Freddie Lindstrom played regularly with Jackson. In 1926, Kelly moved to first and Frankie Frisch took over at second. In 1927, Terry returned to first, with Rogers Hornsby replacing Frisch at second.

Jackson's ideal lineup includes two non-contemporaries—Mantle and Musial—and four American League contemporaries—Cronin, Di-Maggio, Cochrane, and Johnson.

Jackson's's choice as his chief mound nemesis was Charlie Root, a righthander who won 201 games in a 17-year career with the Browns (1923) and Cubs (1926-41).

TRAVIS JACKSON
NEW YORK GIANTS – SHORTSTOP 1924

Jackson's election to Cooperstown completed the only three all-Hall-of-Fame infields.

Career Highlights
Lifetime batting average: .291
Hall of Fame: 1982

THE ULTIMATE LINEUP ACCORDING TO
Ferguson Jenkins

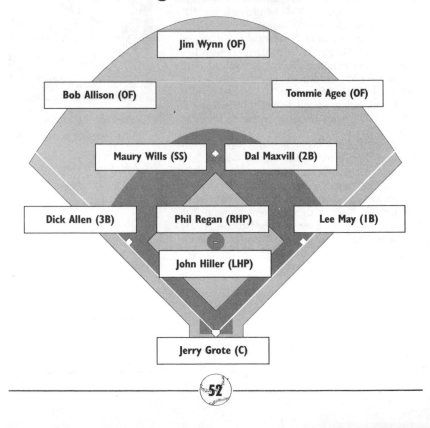

Jim Wynn (OF)

Bob Allison (OF)

Tommie Agee (OF)

Maury Wills (SS)

Dal Maxvill (2B)

Dick Allen (3B)

Phil Regan (RHP)

Lee May (1B)

John Hiller (LHP)

Jerry Grote (C)

JENKINS IS THE ONLY PITCHER in baseball history to strike out more than 3,000 batters and walk fewer than 1,000, a combination that ranks him second to Juan Marichal for the best ratio of strikeouts to walks. He spent his 19-year career in both leagues—with the Phillies (1965-66), Cubs (1966-73, 1982-83), Rangers (1974-75, 1978-81), and Red Sox (1976-77).

The right-hander won at least 20 games for six consecutive seasons (1967-72) with the Cubs, and in 1971 he captured the Cy Young Award for his 24 wins. Jenkins also led the American League in victories with 25 in 1974. He finished his career in 1983 with an overall record of 284-226 and an ERA of 3.34.

Jenkins names Pete Rose as his toughest out. "You got a couple of strikes on him sometimes, it was like he had three balls on you. He also had a great talent for just poking or slapping at very good pitches and driving them to the opposite field. He could be very frustrating."

Most underrated player? "I played with him for a long time—Billy Williams. Sometimes it was like he was turning out all those great numbers of his in a closet. Nobody ever seemed to notice."

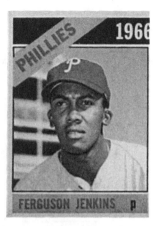

Jenkins contends that his toughest out was Pete Rose.

Career Highlights
284 wins
Posted 7 20-win seasons
3,192 strikeouts
Cy Young Award: 1971
Hall of Fame: 1991

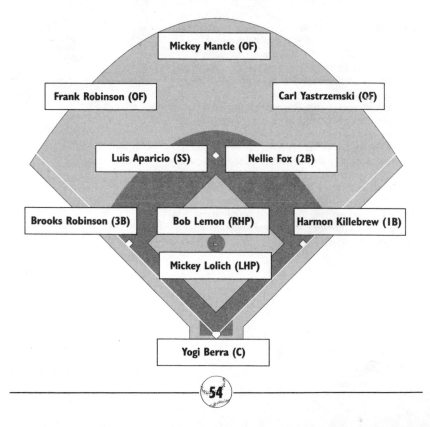

THE ULTIMATE LINEUP ACCORDING TO

Al Kaline

Mickey Mantle (OF)

Frank Robinson (OF)

Carl Yastrzemski (OF)

Luis Aparicio (SS)

Nellie Fox (2B)

Brooks Robinson (3B)

Bob Lemon (RHP)

Harmon Killebrew (1B)

Mickey Lolich (LHP)

Yogi Berra (C)

KALINE HIT .297 WITH 399 home runs in 22 years (1953-74) for the Tigers. The righthand-hitting outfielder amassed 3,007 hits during his career, and at one time or another led the American League in batting (1955), hits (1955), slugging percentage (1959), and doubles (1961). He was also recognized for his strong defensive abilities, netting 10 Golden Glove Awards.

His best seasons were 1955, (.340, 27 home runs, 102 runs batted in, and 121 runs scored) and 1956, (.314, 27 home runs, 128 runs batted in, 96 runs scored).

Never having had to hit against Lolich and aside from Lemon, Kaline considers Early Wynn and Nolan Ryan the toughest pitchers he had to face. "I would have to distinguish between them, because I regarded Lemon and Wynn as the most difficult when I was a good hitter. By the time Ryan came into the league, I was well past it."

Kaline considers longtime teammate Norm Cash the most underrated player from his era. "He hit and hit with power, but he gets lost in the shuffle all the time. You have to put Killebrew somewhere, and that's the only reason I'd pick him ahead of Cash. I've always liked reminding people that, in 1961, when Roger Maris beat Babe Ruth's record— and Mickey Mantle also came close to beating it— Cash and Rocky Colavito on our club actually drove in more runs than they did as a one-two punch—272 to 270."

In Kaline's opinion, teammate Norm Cash was the most underrated player of his time.

Career Highlights
399 home runs
3.007 hits
Hall of Fame: 1980

THE ULTIMATE LINEUP ACCORDING TO
George Kell

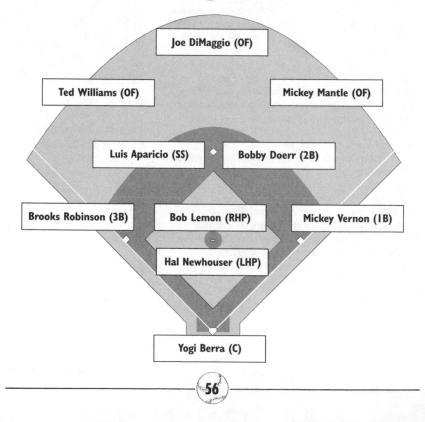

Joe DiMaggio (OF)

Ted Williams (OF)

Mickey Mantle (OF)

Luis Aparicio (SS)

Bobby Doerr (2B)

Brooks Robinson (3B)

Bob Lemon (RHP)

Mickey Vernon (1B)

Hal Newhouser (LHP)

Yogi Berra (C)

THIRD BASEMAN KELL had a 15-year American League career that included stints with the Athletics (1943-46), Tigers (1946-52), Red Sox (1952-54), White Sox (1954-56), and Orioles (1956-57).

A career .306 hitter, Kell won the American League batting title in 1949 with a .343 average and hit over .300 for eight consecutive seasons (1946-53). In 1950 and 1951, he led the league in both hits and doubles. Perhaps his most productive day came on September 20, 1946, when he stroked six hits in a single game.

Kell would put one asterisk next to his ideal lineup. "Lemon was probably the number one money pitcher of my time, but he also came in a Cleveland package with Bob Feller, Early Wynn, and Mike Garcia that was easily the most daunting rotation around. The only time you didn't get one of them going against you was maybe the second game of a Sunday doubleheader."

He would also make room for Gil McDougald of the Yankees. "He was probably the most under-rated player of the 1950s because Casey Stengel always had him moving from second base to shortstop to third base. But he was not what we call today a utility infielder. When he played second, he was one of the best in the league there, and the same thing was true of short and third. Eventually, all that moving around seemed to affect his hitting, but I for one never wanted to see him up at bat with the game in the balance."

Kell considers Bob Lemon the premier "money pitcher" of the era.

Career Highlights
Batting Crown: 1949
Hall of Fame: 1983

THE ULTIMATE LINEUP ACCORDING TO
Harmon Killebrew

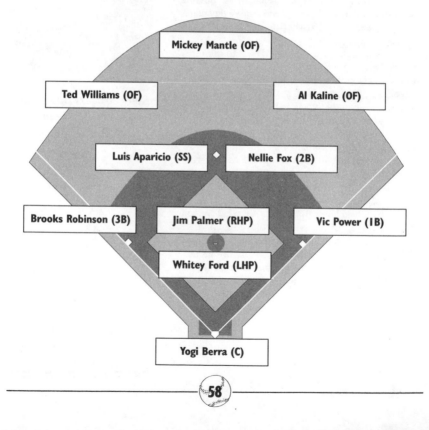

Mickey Mantle (OF)

Ted Williams (OF)

Al Kaline (OF)

Luis Aparicio (SS)

Nellie Fox (2B)

Brooks Robinson (3B)

Jim Palmer (RHP)

Vic Power (1B)

Whitey Ford (LHP)

Yogi Berra (C)

THE GREATEST RIGHTHANDED power hitter in American League history, Killebrew clouted 573 home runs with a .256 average in 21 years with the Washington Senators-Minnesota Twins (1954-74) and a final season (1975) with the Kansas City Royals. His numerous achievements include leading the league in home runs six times, in runs batted in three times, and in slugging percentage twice.

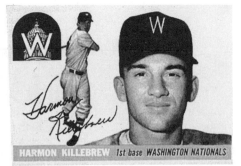

HARMON KILLEBREW 1st base WASHINGTON NATIONALS

A first baseman, third baseman, and outfielder, Killebrew collected eight seasons with at least 40 homers, drove in more than 100 runs nine times, and drew at least 100 walks seven times. His single best season was 1969, when he won the Most Valuable Player award for clubbing 49 homers, driving in 140 runs, walking 145 times, and batting .276. He ranks behind only Babe Ruth and Ralph Kiner for the best ratio of home runs per at bats and has the odd distinction of never having sacrificed in 2,435 games.

Killebrew singles out Power as his most unlikely choice, "though it has always surprised me how many people have forgotten what a wizard he was defensively."

The teammate he remembers as never having received enough credit is Cesar Tovar. "The man was a dream to hit behind. A truly great leadoff man who always seemed to be on base and who distracted the pitcher enough to benefit everyone who batted behind him."

Asked who was his most difficult pitcher, Killebrew skips the better known names to select Stu Miller. "He was always slow, slower, and still slower, and I never seemed to be quite slow enough."

Career Highlights
573 home runs
Most Valuable Player: 1969
Hall of Fame: 1984

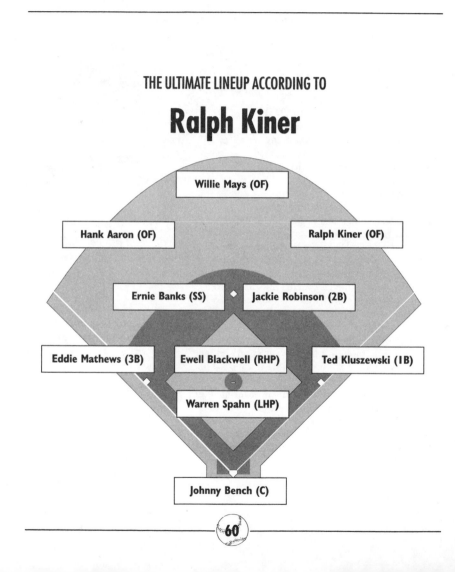

THE ULTIMATE LINEUP ACCORDING TO

Ralph Kiner

Willie Mays (OF)

Hank Aaron (OF)

Ralph Kiner (OF)

Ernie Banks (SS)

Jackie Robinson (2B)

Eddie Mathews (3B)

Ewell Blackwell (RHP)

Ted Kluszewski (1B)

Warren Spahn (LHP)

Johnny Bench (C)

ALTHOUGH HE PLAYED FOR ONLY 10 years, Kiner clouted 369 homers, leading or tying for the National League lead in that category in his first seven seasons (1946-52). Over that period, the righthand-hitting outfielder was the Pittsburgh franchise as much as any player has ever dominated a team. Despite the fact that the Pirates had merely one winning season during his tenure, he also led the league in runs batted in and slugging three times.

Kiner's best season was 1949, when he batted .310, stroked 54 homers, drove in 127 runs, and had a slugging percentage of .658. He closed out his career with a lifetime .279 average, after a season and a half with the Cubs and an injury-plagued year with the Indians.

Kiner has never concealed his awe of Ewell Blackwell, a pitcher with only an 82-78 career record. "His delivery was unorthodox. He looked like a man falling out of a tree. It was hard to pick up the ball, and since you only had about two-fifths of a second to react, it was next to impossible to hit it well even when you did pick it up."

Kiner's toughest calls are at shortstop and behind the plate. "There were certainly better defensive shortstops than Banks, but I have to pick him as much for his spirit as for his bat. I would favor Bench very narrowly over Roy Campanella." But one call is not so tough. "If I have to win one game, I want something to say about it myself, so I've got to be in there."

TURN BACK THE CLOCK

25 YRS. AGO-1952

KINER LEADS N.L. FOR 7th STRAIGHT YEAR

In his short 10-year career, Kiner finished second only to Babe Ruth in home runs per at bat.

Career Highlights
369 home runs
Led league in home runs seven times
Hall of Fame: 1975

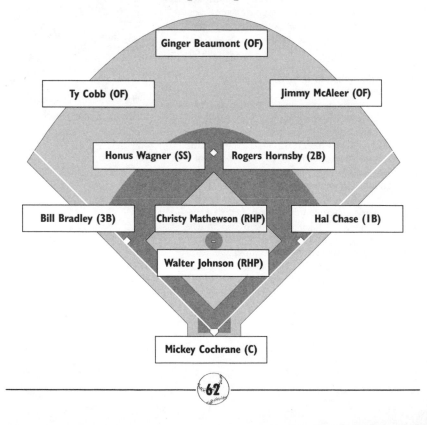

THE ULTIMATE LINEUP ACCORDING TO

Nap Lajoie

Ginger Beaumont (OF)

Ty Cobb (OF)

Jimmy McAleer (OF)

Honus Wagner (SS)

Rogers Hornsby (2B)

Bill Bradley (3B)

Christy Mathewson (RHP)

Hal Chase (1B)

Walter Johnson (RHP)

Mickey Cochrane (C)

LAJOIE WAS BASEBALL'S greatest second base-man before Rogers Hornsby, batting .338 in 21 seasons (1896-1916) with the Philadelphia Phillies, Philadelphia Athletics, and Cleveland Indians. His .422 average with the A's in 1901 is the highest ever recorded by an American League player and second in the 20th century only to Hornsby's .424. He also led the league in batting in 1903 and 1904, in doubles four times, in hits four times, and in homers once. The righthanded hitter was also considered the American League's best glove at second base for a good part of his career. During his five seasons as Cleveland's manager (1905-09), the team was known as the Naps.

Lajoie's lineup includes two righthanded pitchers, but no lefty, and three players not normally associated with all-time dream lineups. Bill Bradley was Cleveland's third baseman in the first decade of the century; he batted .271 over a 14-year career. Jimmy McAleer was a lifetime .255 hitter with a great glove and was considered the sparkplug of the National League Cleveland Spiders in the 1890s. Ginger Beaumont was a prototypical leadoff man, who scored more than 100 runs five times and led the National League in batting for Pittsburgh in 1902 with a .357 average. Although first baseman Chase had few equals at his position, particularly on defense, in the early years of the century, he has become better known for the numerous accusations leveled against him for throwing games—charges that eventually led to his ouster from baseball.

In 1901, Lajoie posted a .422 batting average, the highest ever recorded by an American League player.

Career Highlights
3,244 hits
.338 lifetime average
Hall of Fame: 1937

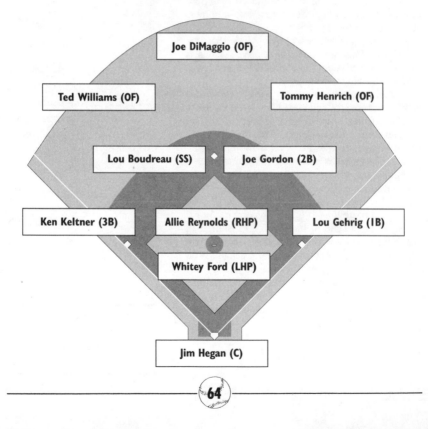

THE ULTIMATE LINEUP ACCORDING TO

Bob Lemon

Joe DiMaggio (OF)

Ted Williams (OF)

Tommy Henrich (OF)

Lou Boudreau (SS)

Joe Gordon (2B)

Ken Keltner (3B)

Allie Reynolds (RHP)

Lou Gehrig (1B)

Whitey Ford (LHP)

Jim Hegan (C)

LEMON, WHO SPENT his entire career with the Indians (1941-42, 1946-58), took to the mound in 1946 after an earlier stint as a third baseman. He ended his career with 207 victories against 128 losses and an ERA of 3.23. A 20-game winner seven times, he led the league in victories three times, complete games five times, innings pitched three times, strikeouts once, and shutouts once. Lemon's best season was 1954, when he led Cleveland to a pennant with a mark of 23-7 and a 2.72 ERA. He also won two games in the 1948 World Series. Following his retirement as a pitcher, the righthander managed the Kansas City Royals, Chicago White Sox, and New York Yankees.

Lemon doesn't apologize for picking five teammates to his lineup—Gordon, Keltner, Boudreau, Hegan, and Reynolds. "Nobody gave me the combination of offense and defense from the middle of the infield that Gordon and Boudreau did. As for Keltner, I always considered him the most overlooked player of the 1940s. Berra may have been a better hitter than Hegan, but nobody in the history of the major leagues could have been a better catcher defensively, and as a pitcher I'm prejudiced about that. Reynolds always won the big game not only for the Indians but especially after we traded him to the Yankees for Gordon."

The player Lemon least wanted to face was Minnie Minoso: "It was the way he stood up at the plate. He didn't care if you hit him to drive in the big run or you threw it away where he could clout it. He was pretty fearless."

Career Highlights
Lifetime record: 207-128
Seven 20-win seasons
Hall of Fame: 1976

THE ULTIMATE LINEUP ACCORDING TO
Buck Leonard

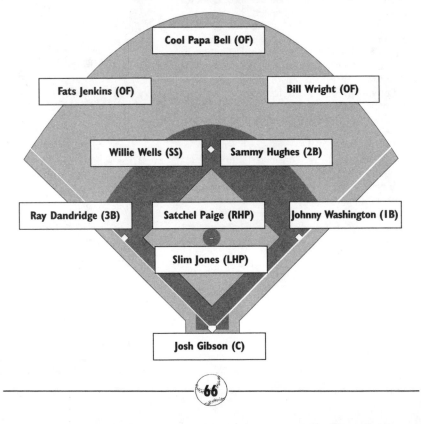

Cool Papa Bell (OF)

Fats Jenkins (OF)

Bill Wright (OF)

Willie Wells (SS)

Sammy Hughes (2B)

Ray Dandridge (3B)

Satchel Paige (RHP)

Johnny Washington (1B)

Slim Jones (LHP)

Josh Gibson (C)

KNOWN AS THE LOU GEHRIG of the Negro Leagues, Leonard played for the Homestead Grays for 17 years (1934-50). Then, after the Negro Leagues folded once Jackie Robinson broke the color barrier, he spent several seasons in the Mexican League and one in the minors.

A lefty-swinging first baseman, Leonard batted about .325 in his career and, with Josh Gibson, formed the power-hitting duo that led the Grays to ten pennants and a record three Negro World Series victories.

Leonard singles out from his lineup shortstop Willie Wells as a much-neglected performer in the Negro Leagues. "People know about Paige and they've heard of Gibson and Bell because they're in the Hall of Fame. But Wells was the best shortstop—black or white—of his time. He was as aggressive—on and off the bases—as Jackie Robinson. He was so good defensively that they called him the Devil, and he could hit like nobody else. I'll wager he hit over .400 against white teams; those exhibition games always brought out the best in him."

Leonard batted about .325 in his career and, with Josh Gibson, formed a legendary power-hitting duo for the Homestead Grays.

Career Highlights
.320-.330 batting average
Three Negro World Series championships
Hall of Fame: 1972

THE ULTIMATE LINEUP ACCORDING TO

Al Lopez

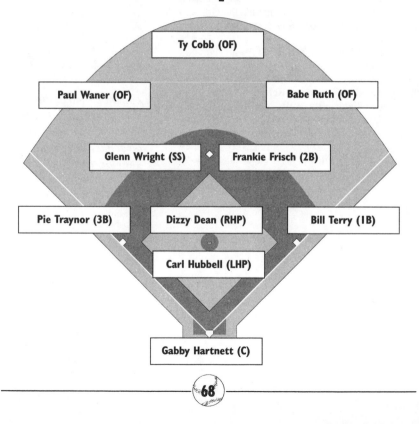

Ty Cobb (OF)

Paul Waner (OF)

Babe Ruth (OF)

Glenn Wright (SS)

Frankie Frisch (2B)

Pie Traynor (3B)

Dizzy Dean (RHP)

Bill Terry (1B)

Carl Hubbell (LHP)

Gabby Hartnett (C)

LOPEZ WAS CONSIDERED the premier defesive catcher in baseball for a good part of his career and held the record for most games by a catcher until he was surpassed in the 1990s by Bob Boone and Carlton Fisk. A .261 lifetime hitter, he had a 19-year career with the Dodgers (1928, 1930-35), Braves (1936-40), Pirates (1940-46), and Indians (1947).

Lopez later managed the Indians (1951-56) and White Sox (1957-65 and parts of 1968 and 1969). He was the only manager to finish ahead of the Yankees in the 1950s: Between 1951 and 1959, his teams never finished below second, and he captured pennants for the Indians in 1954 and the White Sox in 1959.

According to Lopez, Rogers Hornsby ranks with Frisch, Al Simmons with Waner, and Dazzy Vance with Dean. He divides the honor of most underrated player between shortstop Glenn Wright and Babe Herman. "Nobody claims that Wright was a better hitter than people like Lou Boudreau, but he still hit far above what shortstops usually do and he was a whiz in the field. Herman was a decent first baseman and outfielder. He had a bum rap with all that nonsense about being hit on the head or on the shoulder whenever he got under a fly ball. It made him sound like a clown, when in fact he was a great hitter."

As for opposition pitchers, he calls Herb Pennock "the most graceful I ever saw. But when it came down to a one-on-one situation, the pitcher I most hated to see out there was Hal Schumacher of the Giants. He had a very fast sinker, a heavy ball that always bore into the batter."

AL LOPEZ
BOSTON BRAVES – CATCHER   1940

Asked which pitchers were his toughest, Lopez recalls Hal Schumacher of the Giants.

Career Highlights
1,918 games caught
Hall of Fame: 1977

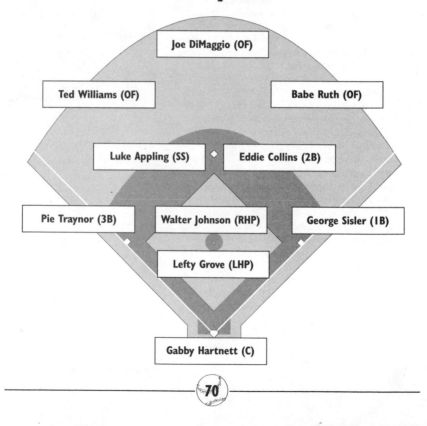

THE ULTIMATE LINEUP ACCORDING TO

Ted Lyons

Joe DiMaggio (OF)

Ted Williams (OF)

Babe Ruth (OF)

Luke Appling (SS)

Eddie Collins (2B)

Pie Traynor (3B)

Walter Johnson (RHP)

George Sisler (1B)

Lefty Grove (LHP)

Gabby Hartnett (C)

RIGHTHANDER LYONS PITCHED for the White Sox for 21 years (1923-42, 1946), compiling a record of 260-230 and a 3.67 ERA for teams that were usually buried in the second division. A three-time 20-game-winner, he also managed the Chicago club from 1946 to 1948.

Lyons names slugger Al Simmons as his tenth player of his lineup. "You have to be Babe Ruth, Ted Williams, or Joe DiMaggio to beat him out. But he gave me a lot of trouble—maybe a little more than he gave other pitchers."

Another nemesis was Boston outfielder Tom Oliver, who batted .277 for the Red Sox between 1930 and 1933. "He owned me," says Lyons. "He always seemed to be punching little hits through the left side, the right side, wherever my infielders weren't."

For the most underrated players of his era, Lyons points to teammates Jackie Hayes, Bibb Falk, and Johnny Mostil: "Hayes was the equal of anyone as a defensive second baseman until his eyes started to go on him, and he was no automatic out, either. Falk and Mostil were both lifetime .300 hitters who got lost in the general mediocrity of the Chicago teams. When you talk about Mostil, in particular, you're talking about one of the greatest defensive outfielders and runners of all time."

Although hardly underrated, Lyons's Hall of Fame batterymate Ray Schalk also comes in for praise. "Defensively he was much better than a lot of others. In one game, he made a putout at every base."

TED LYONS
CHICAGO WHITE SOX – PITCHER   1932

Lyons points to teammates Jackie Hayes, Bibb Falk, and Johnny Mostil as some of the most underrated players of his era.

Career Highlights
260 wins
Led league in victories twice
Hall of Fame: 1955

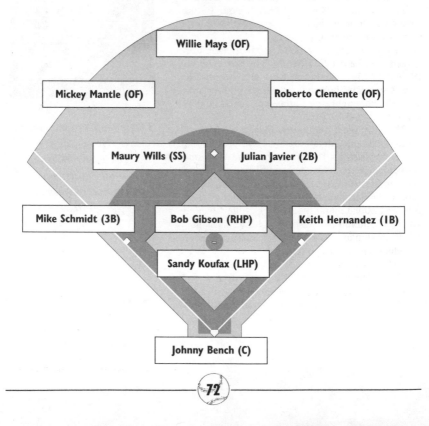

THE ULTIMATE LINEUP ACCORDING TO

Juan Marichal

- Willie Mays (OF)
- Mickey Mantle (OF)
- Roberto Clemente (OF)
- Maury Wills (SS)
- Julian Javier (2B)
- Mike Schmidt (3B)
- Bob Gibson (RHP)
- Keith Hernandez (1B)
- Sandy Koufax (LHP)
- Johnny Bench (C)

DURING HIS 15-YEAR CAREER, Marichal posted a record of 243-142 and a 2.89 ERA, mostly with the San Francisco Giants. He won more than 20 games six times, struck out more than 200 batters six times, and hurled 52 shutouts. The righthander's single-game accomplishments include retiring the first 19 batters he faced in his 1960 debut and pitching a no-hitter in 1963. Among his best seasons were 1963 (25-8, 2.41), 1966 (25-6, 2.23), 1968 (26-9, 2.43), and 1969 (a league-leading 2.10 ERA). A master of control, Marichal holds the major league record for strike-out-walk ratio, with 3.27 strikeouts per base on balls. One of the anomalies of Marichal's career is that, despite his powerful single-season marks, he never won a Cy Young Award. He closed out his major league endeavors with brief stints with the Red Sox and the Dodgers.

Marichal notes that his choice of a first baseman to his lineup might surprise some, especially since Hernandez came along after he retired. "I played with great first baseman like Orlando Cepeda and Willie McCovey, but as a pitcher I would want Hernandez behind me. No one I have ever seen has played the position like he did."

He also admits to a temptation to stick Cal Ripken at shortstop instead of Maury Wills. "But when it comes down to it, maybe the ideal solution is just to take the Big Red Machine teams of Cincinnati in the 1970s. With them I would have won 30 games a year *minimum*. In fact, I told the Giants once to trade me to the Reds on the condition that I wouldn't get paid until I'd won my thirty-first game. Then I would've soaked them."

Marichal, who often had the bad fortune to compete against Sandy Koufax for top pitching honors in the National League, never won a Cy Young Award.

Career Highlights
Six 20-win seasons
Lifetime record: 243-142
Hall of Fame: 1983

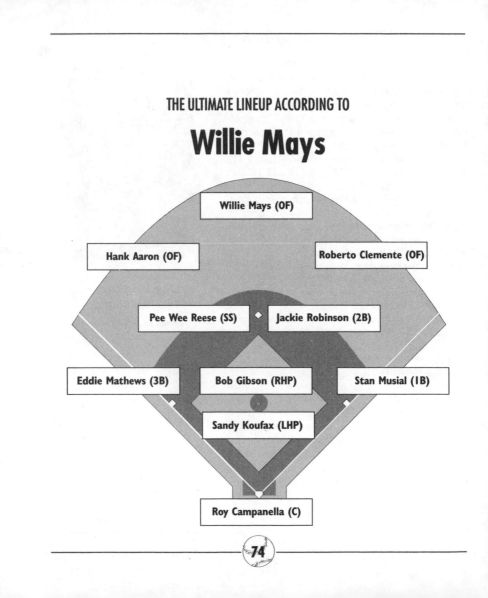

THE ULTIMATE LINEUP ACCORDING TO

Willie Mays

Willie Mays (OF)

Hank Aaron (OF)

Roberto Clemente (OF)

Pee Wee Reese (SS)

Jackie Robinson (2B)

Eddie Mathews (3B)

Bob Gibson (RHP)

Stan Musial (1B)

Sandy Koufax (LHP)

Roy Campanella (C)

PERHAPS THE SINGLE most exciting player of his generation, Mays batted .302 over 22 seasons with the New York and San Francisco versions of the Giants (1951-1952, 1954-1972) and the New York Mets (1972-73). The righthanded-hitting outfielder ranks ninth on the all-time list in hits, seventh in runs batted in, sixth in games played, fifth in runs scored, and third in total bases. Mays also hit 660 career home runs, which places him behind only Ruth and Aaron.

Mays led the National League in batting once, runs scored twice, stolen bases four times, and home runs four times. On April 30, 1961, he joined the handful of sluggers who have hit four home runs in a single game. A defensive whiz known for spectacular basket catches, he earned twelve consecutive Gold Gloves between 1957 and 1968.

Along with Gibson and Koufax, Mays mentioned Don Drysdale of the Dodgers as a pitcher who gave him particular trouble. Also on Mays's personal least-favorite list was the unsung Bob Rush of the Cubs and Braves. "I just couldn't pick up his pitches. Later on, I learned that he had a problem with his eyes, so it's a wonder he could pitch at all. If I'd known that when I was facing him, I might have been even more awkward up there."

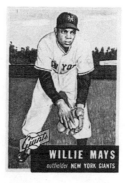

Asked to identify the most underrated player of his time, Mays singles out Hank Aaron. ". . . he never got the attention he deserved for being the great all-around player that he was. He could run, throw, hit to the opposite field, do it all."

Career Highlights
3,283 hits
1.903 runs batted in
660 home runs
Rookie of the Year: 1951
Most Valuable Player: 1954, 1965
Hall of Fame: 1979

75

THE ULTIMATE LINEUP ACCORDING TO
Willie McCovey

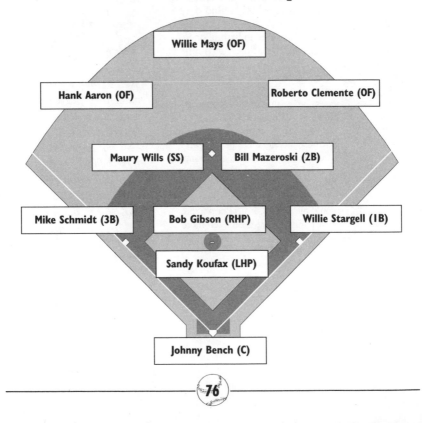

Willie Mays (OF)

Hank Aaron (OF)

Roberto Clemente (OF)

Maury Wills (SS)

Bill Mazeroski (2B)

Mike Schmidt (3B)

Bob Gibson (RHP)

Willie Stargell (1B)

Sandy Koufax (LHP)

Johnny Bench (C)

MCCOVEY CRACKED 521 home runs in a 22-year career with the Giants (1959-73), Padres (1974-76), Athletics (1976), and Giants again (1977-80). A lifetime .270 hitter, the lefty-swinging first baseman led the National League in homers three times, slugging three times, runs batted in twice, and walks once. He stands second on the all-time list in grand-slam home runs with 18 and is tied for third in pinch-hit home runs with 16. In seven different years, he blasted at least 30 homers.

McCovey's single most productive season was 1969, when he took Most Valuable Player honors for batting .320 with 45 homers, 26 doubles, 121 walks, 126 runs batted in, and 101 runs scored. He also won Rookie-of-the-Year recognition in 1959.

Hank Aaron, McCovey insists, never received enough recognition during his playing days. "Part of the problem was the home run thing, which was great, but which turned attention away from what a complete player he was. Another thing was that he played in relatively small cities like Milwaukee and Atlanta. If he'd been on a team like the Yankees, everyone would've known about him long before he came near Ruth's record."

McCovey doesn't have to think twice about the toughest pitcher he had to face. "That has to be Bob Veale of the Pirates. It wasn't just because he was a southpaw, either, because he had fabulous stuff. He could've been throwing with his right hand just for me, and I still don't think I would've hit him."

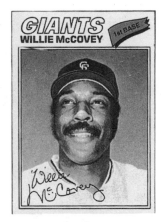

McCovey insists that Hank Aaron never received enough recognition during his playing days: ". . . the home run thing . . . turned attention away from what a complete player he was."

Career Highlights
521 home runs
Rookie of the Year: 1959
Most Valuable Player: 1969
Hall of Fame: 1986

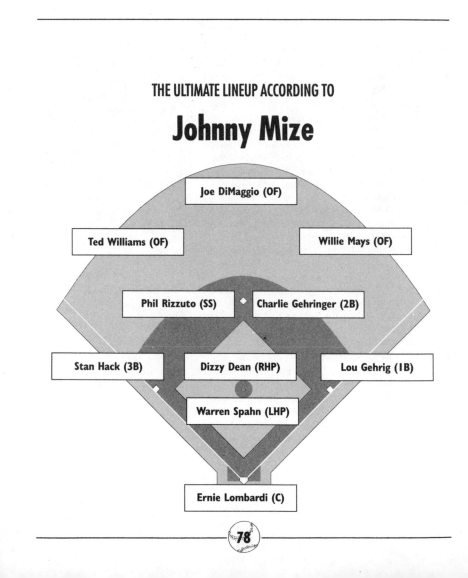

THE ULTIMATE LINEUP ACCORDING TO

Johnny Mize

Joe DiMaggio (OF)

Ted Williams (OF)

Willie Mays (OF)

Phil Rizzuto (SS)

Charlie Gehringer (2B)

Stan Hack (3B)

Dizzy Dean (RHP)

Lou Gehrig (1B)

Warren Spahn (LHP)

Ernie Lombardi (C)

MIZE LED OR TIED for the National League lead in home runs in 1939, 1940, 1947, and 1948, and also topped the senior circuit in runs batted in three times and slugging four times. The lefty-hitting first baseman batted .312 with 359 home runs playing for the Cardinals (1936-41), Giants 1942, 1946-49), and Yankees (1949-53).

No wallop-or-whiff batter, Mize also won the hitting crown in 1939 with a .349 mark, and went as high as .364 in 1937. He hit three homers in a game six times, a major league record. After being picked up by the Yankees in 1949, he played in five straight World Series, clubbing three homers in the 1952 Series.

Mize's bench would include Stan Musial, Jimmie Foxx, Pee Wee Reese, Gabby Hartnett, Bill Dickey, and Bob Feller. "You wouldn't do too badly with them instead of the ones I picked." As for his selection of Stan Hack over better-known third basemen: "He was probably the most underrated player in the 1930s because the Cubs weren't always the greatest team in the league. But he could hit and field, and he was in there every day." (Hack batted .301 in 16 seasons with Chicago.)

His toughest pitcher was "unquestionably Russ Bauers. He was a tall righthander with a big curve that started up near your eyes, then zoomed down when it reached you." (Bauers won 31 against 30 defeats in eight seasons with the Pirates, Cubs, and Browns. He had a career ERA of 2.88.)

JOHNNY MIZE
ST. LOUIS CARDINALS – 1ST BASE   1936

Mize's toughest pitcher was "unquestionably" Russ Bauers.

Career Highlights
Six three-homer games
359 home runs
Lifetime batting average: .312
Hall of Fame: 1981

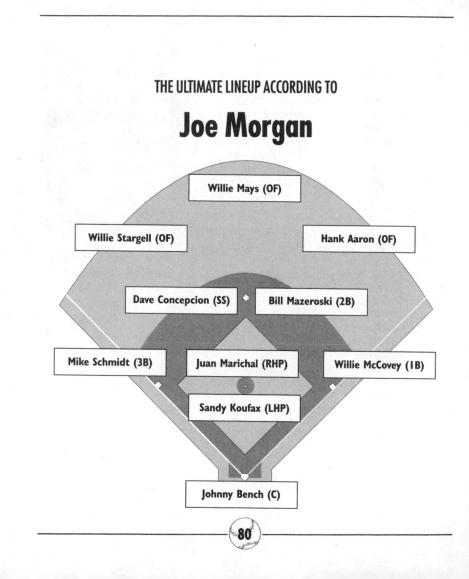

THE ULTIMATE LINEUP ACCORDING TO

Joe Morgan

Willie Mays (OF)

Willie Stargell (OF)

Hank Aaron (OF)

Dave Concepcion (SS)

Bill Mazeroski (2B)

Mike Schmidt (3B)

Juan Marichal (RHP)

Willie McCovey (1B)

Sandy Koufax (LHP)

Johnny Bench (C)

FEW PLAYERS ACHIEVED a reputation for being a winner as firmly as Morgan did during his 22 years with the Astros (1963-71, 1980), Reds (1972-79), Giants (1981-82), Phillies (1983), and Athletics (1984). A perennial force for contending or pennant-winning teams, the lefthanded hitter holds the National League record for walks. Also, his 266 home runs as a second baseman (out of a career total of 268) is the major league high for that position. Morgan closed his career with a .271 average and 689 stolen bases.

In both 1975 and 1976, Morgan was named Most Valuable Player—in the former year for batting .327 with 17 homers, 27 doubles, 94 runs batted in, 107 runs, 132 walks, and 67 steals; in the latter for hitting .320 with 27 home runs, 30 doubles, 111 runs batted in, 113 runs scored, and 60 steals.

According to Morgan, McCovey is a tough call over Big Red Machine teammate Tony Perez at first base. "He wasn't as noticed as much as me, Rose, or Bench, and I think that's mainly because we could talk better. When you're talking about underrated players, you're talking about players who didn't establish an entertaining relationship with the media. In that sense, Tony qualifies as underrated, but not because his teammates or the players around the league didn't realize how good he was."

Morgan picks out New York Mets southpaw Jon Matlack as his most difficult mound adversary. "He always kept me uncomfortable, and he knew what he was doing every minute, every pitch."

Career Highlights
268 home runs
689 stolen bases
Most Valuable Player: 1975, 1976
Hall of Fame: 1990

THE ULTIMATE LINEUP ACCORDING TO
Hal Newhouser

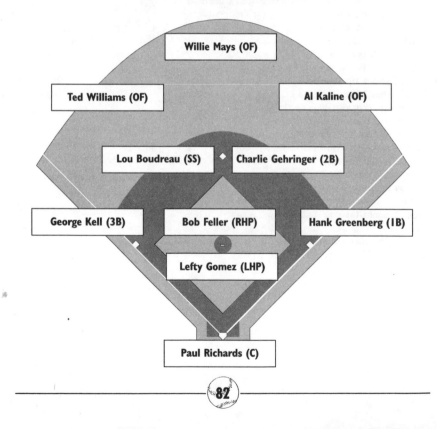

Willie Mays (OF)

Ted Williams (OF)

Al Kaline (OF)

Lou Boudreau (SS)

Charlie Gehringer (2B)

George Kell (3B)

Bob Feller (RHP)

Hank Greenberg (1B)

Lefty Gomez (LHP)

Paul Richards (C)

THE ULTIMATE LINEUP ACCORDING TO

Phil Rizzuto

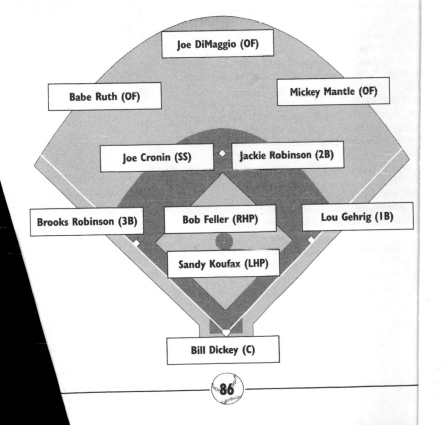

Joe DiMaggio (OF)

Babe Ruth (OF)

Mickey Mantle (OF)

Joe Cronin (SS)

Jackie Robinson (2B)

Brooks Robinson (3B)

Bob Feller (RHP)

Lou Gehrig (1B)

Sandy Koufax (LHP)

Bill Dickey (C)

THE PREMIER SOUTHPAW in the American League for most of the 1940s, Newhouser had a career record of 207-150 and a 3.06 ERA in 15 seasons (1939-53) with the Tigers and two more (1954-55) with the Indians. Between 1944 and 1948, he led the league in victories four times, with 29 in 1944, in ERA and strikeouts twice, and in shutouts and winning percentage once. His records in 1944 (with 29-9, 2.22 ERA, 187 strikeouts, and 6 shutouts) and 1945 (with 25-9, 1.81 ERA, 212 strikeouts, and 8 shutouts) enabled him to become the only pitcher to win back-to-back Most Valuable Player awards.

To back up his lineup, Newhouser would include Stan Musial at first base; Joe Gordon and Bobby Doerr at second; Phil Rizzuto, Luis Aparicio, and Marty Marion at shortstop; Bill Dickey behind the plate; and Robin Roberts, Sandy Koufax, Whitey Ford, and himself on the mound.

Despite picking an outfield of Kaline, Williams, and Mays, Newhouser describes Joe DiMaggio as his toughest out. "Everyone knows what a great player he was, but he never really had a weakness I could take advantage of with any consistency."

With regard to his catching choice, he admits that "it would be easier if Richards had hit .300," but insists that no other backstop of his era was better defensively.

HAL NEWHOUSER
DETROIT TIGERS – PITCHER
1940

Newhouser lead the league in victories four times, in ERA and strikeouts twice, and in shutouts and winning percentage once.

Career Highlights
Most Valuable Player: 1944, 1945
Lifetime record: 207-150
Hall of Fame: 1992

THE ULTIMATE LINEUP ACCORDING TO
Pee Wee Reese

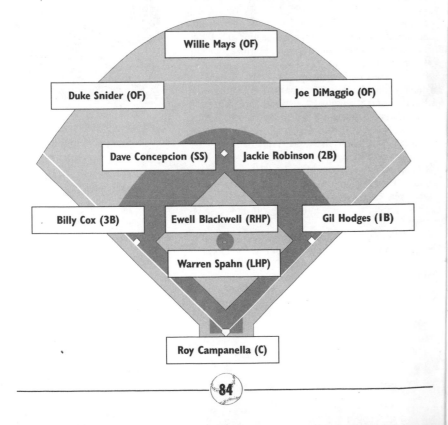

Willie Mays (OF)

Duke Snider (OF)

Joe DiMaggio (OF)

Dave Concepcion (SS)

Jackie Robinson (2B)

Billy Cox (3B)

Ewell Blackwell (RHP)

Gil Hodges (1B)

Warren Spahn (LHP)

Roy Campanella (C)

THE FIELD CAPTAIN and heart of the Boys of Summer teams that played in Brooklyn, Reese batted .269 in a 16-year career with the Dodgers (1940-42, 1946-58). Aside from his defensive skill at shortstop, he led the National League at one time or another in walks, stolen bases, and runs scored. His most productive offensive seasons were 1949, when he batted .279 with 16 home runs and 132 runs scored, and 1951, when he drove home 84 runs, despite hitting second in the lineup.

Reese admits to an asterisk in his choice of Spahn as the southpaw in his lineup. "The fact of the matter is, the Dodger teams I played on killed him whenever he pitched against us. We had so many righthanded hitters who ate up lefties that they eventually stopped pitching him against us, especially at Ebbets Field. Still, I don't think that should detract from the fact that he won more games than any other lefty in baseball history. This time we'd be on his side!"

As for the righty Blackwell, he goes along with other National League right-handed hitters of the period who found him "unhittable at times."

The single greatest player he ever saw? "DiMaggio. He did it all, and he did it so gracefully."

PEE WEE REESE
Pee Wee "Reese"

Reese contends that the most underrated player his time was Carl Fu...

"No question. We... lot of great hitter... the clutch he... with Jackie R... defensively... having o... fielder w...

THE PREMIER SOUTHPAW in the American League for most of the 1940s, Newhouser had a career record of 207-150 and a 3.06 ERA in 15 seasons (1939-53) with the Tigers and two more (1954-55) with the Indians. Between 1944 and 1948, he led the league in victories four times, with 29 in 1944, in ERA and strikeouts twice, and in shutouts and winning percentage once. His records in 1944 (with 29-9, 2.22 ERA, 187 strikeouts, and 6 shutouts) and 1945 (with 25-9, 1.81 ERA, 212 strikeouts, and 8 shutouts) enabled him to become the only pitcher to win back-to-back Most Valuable Player awards.

To back up his lineup, Newhouser would include Stan Musial at first base; Joe Gordon and Bobby Doerr at second; Phil Rizzuto, Luis Aparicio, and Marty Marion at shortstop; Bill Dickey behind the plate; and Robin Roberts, Sandy Koufax, Whitey Ford, and himself on the mound.

Despite picking an outfield of Kaline, Williams, and Mays, Newhouser describes Joe DiMaggio as his toughest out. "Everyone knows what a great player he was, but he never really had a weakness I could take advantage of with any consistency."

With regard to his catching choice, he admits that "it would be easier if Richards had hit .300," but insists that no other backstop of his era was better defensively.

HAL NEWHOUSER
DETROIT TIGERS · PITCHER · 1940

Newhouser lead the league in victories four times, in ERA and strikeouts twice, and in shutouts and winning percentage once.

Career Highlights
Most Valuable Player: 1944, 1945
Lifetime record: 207-150
Hall of Fame: 1992

THE ULTIMATE LINEUP ACCORDING TO
Pee Wee Reese

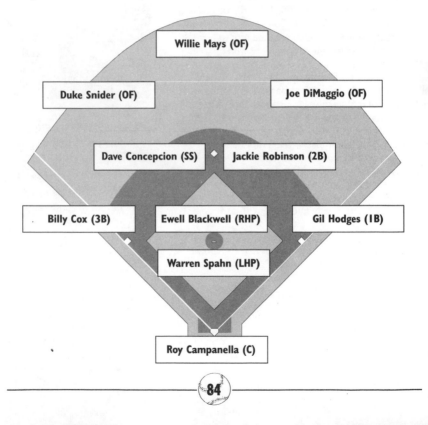

Willie Mays (OF)

Duke Snider (OF)

Joe DiMaggio (OF)

Dave Concepcion (SS)

Jackie Robinson (2B)

Billy Cox (3B)

Ewell Blackwell (RHP)

Gil Hodges (1B)

Warren Spahn (LHP)

Roy Campanella (C)

THE FIELD CAPTAIN and heart of the Boys of Summer teams that played in Brooklyn, Reese batted .269 in a 16-year career with the Dodgers (1940-42, 1946-58). Aside from his defensive skill at shortstop, he led the National League at one time or another in walks, stolen bases, and runs scored. His most productive offensive seasons were 1949, when he batted .279 with 16 home runs and 132 runs scored, and 1951, when he drove home 84 runs, despite hitting second in the lineup.

Reese admits to an asterisk in his choice of Spahn as the southpaw in his lineup. "The fact of the matter is, the Dodger teams I played on killed him whenever he pitched against us. We had so many righthanded hitters who ate up lefties that they eventually stopped pitching him against us, especially at Ebbets Field. Still, I don't think that should detract from the fact that he won more games than any other lefty in baseball history. This time we'd be on his side!"

As for the righty Blackwell, he goes along with other National League right-handed hitters of the period who found him "unhittable at times."

The single greatest player he ever saw? "DiMaggio. He did it all, and he did it so gracefully."

Reese contends that the most underrated player of his time was Carl Furillo. "No question. We had a lot of great hitters, but in the clutch he was there with Jackie Robinson. And defensively it was like having another center fielder with a great arm."

Career Highlights
232 stolen bases
Lifetime batting average: .269
Hall of Fame: 1984

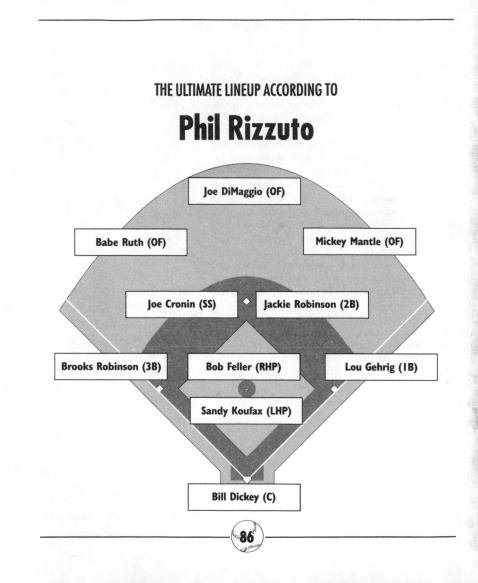

THE ULTIMATE LINEUP ACCORDING TO

Phil Rizzuto

Joe DiMaggio (OF)

Babe Ruth (OF)

Mickey Mantle (OF)

Joe Cronin (SS)

Jackie Robinson (2B)

Brooks Robinson (3B)

Bob Feller (RHP)

Lou Gehrig (1B)

Sandy Koufax (LHP)

Bill Dickey (C)

AMONG THE MOST POPULAR base-ball personalities, Rizzuto hit .273 in 13 years with the Yankees (1941-42, 1946-56) and was considered the premier American League shortstop of his era. A bunting spe-cialist, the righthanded hitter twice batted over .300 and twice scored more than 100 runs per season. In 1950, his personal sea-son highs in batting (.324), hits (200), dou-bles (36), runs scored (125), slugging average (.439) and walks (92) earned him the American League Most Valuable Player award. A longtime Yankee television an-nouncer, "The Scooter" has spent more than a half century with the New York club on the field and in the TV booth.

shortstop NEW YORK YANKEES

Rizzuto's selections span generations. "The last time I was asked to pick an all-star team I forgot Babe Ruth. I said then, 1957, that I would never pick another. But there I go again, leaving out Ted Wil liams. I hope Ted will forgive. I'm prejudiced for Yan-kees, I guess. DiMag was the best I played with, and Mickey was right behind him. And just because I never played with the Babe—or Lou Gehrig, either, for that matter—is no reason not to have the two best hitters ever on my team."

Rizzuto's toughest pitcher? "Every time I thought I had Feller's fastball timed he would blink at me and one of those big overhand curves of his would come out of the white shirts in center field and I'd be out again."

Rizzuto says that the most underrated player of his time is a Yankee teammate: "Tommy Henrich was a great outfielder and an even better clutch hitter. He carried us when other guys were hurt."

Career Highlights
Most Valuable Player: 1950
Lifetime batting average: .273
Hall of Fame: 1994

THE ULTIMATE LINEUP ACCORDING TO
Brooks Robinson

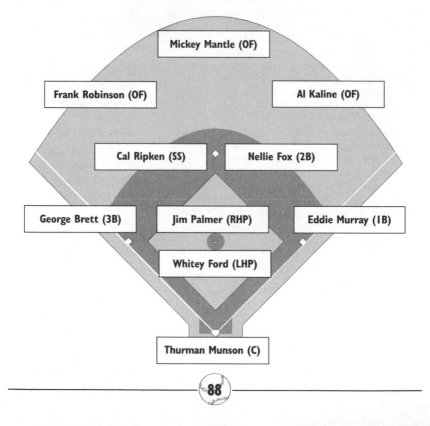

Mickey Mantle (OF)

Frank Robinson (OF)

Al Kaline (OF)

Cal Ripken (SS)

Nellie Fox (2B)

George Brett (3B)

Jim Palmer (RHP)

Eddie Murray (1B)

Whitey Ford (LHP)

Thurman Munson (C)

PROBABLY THE GREATEST defensive third baseman in the history of the game, Robinson spent his entire 23-year career as an Oriole (1955-77), batting .267 with 268 home runs. His best year with the bat was his Most Valuable Player season of 1964, when he hit .317 with 28 home runs, 35 doubles, and a league-leading 118 runs batted in. That was one of six seasons in which he hit at least 20 home runs. His fielding superiority earned him 16 straight Golden Gloves, and he heads the lists of all third baseman in career games, putouts, assists, double plays, and fielding percentage. His acrobatics in the 1970 World Series offered a national showcase in infield defense.

Robinson singles out righthanders Frank Lary and Earl Wilson as the pitchers who gave him the most trouble. "Let's just say that fast balls in and sliders from righties were not my favorite thing when I was hitting, and they were both expert at it."

"When you're talking about underrated players, the one guy who should be mentioned by anybody who was in the game when I was is Paul Blair. He was the greatest center fielder I ever saw defensively, and he was no slouch at the plate."

Robinson singles out righthanders Frank Lary and Earl Wilson as the pitchers who gave him the most trouble.

Career Highlights

2,870 games at third base

2,697 putouts

618 double plays

6,205 assists

.971 fielding average

Most Valuable Player: 1964

Hall of Fame: 1983

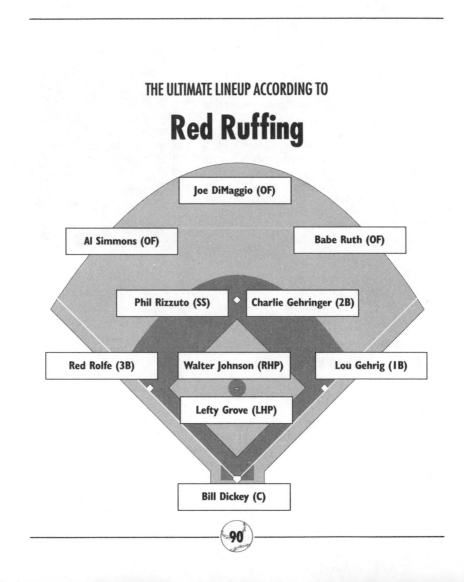

THE ULTIMATE LINEUP ACCORDING TO

Red Ruffing

Joe DiMaggio (OF)

Al Simmons (OF)

Babe Ruth (OF)

Phil Rizzuto (SS)

Charlie Gehringer (2B)

Red Rolfe (3B)

Walter Johnson (RHP)

Lou Gehrig (1B)

Lefty Grove (LHP)

Bill Dickey (C)

RIGHT-HANDER RUFFING PUT together a record of 273 wins against 225 losses and an ERA of 3.80 over 22 seasons with the Red Sox (1924-30), Yankees (1930-42, 1945-47), and White Sox (1947). The most astonishing thing about his career is that, while with Boston, his 39-96 ranked him among the worst in baseball history; traded to the Bronx, however, he won 231 against only 124 losses.

A four-time 20-game winner for New York, Ruffing led the American League in strikeouts in 1932, in wins and winning percentage in 1938, and in shutouts in both 1938 and 1939. One of the best hitting pitchers of all time, he batted higher than .300 eight times and knocked 36 homers, good for third place among pitchers. Between 1936 and 1939, he showed remarkable consistency in posting mound records of 20-12, 20-7, 21-7, and 21-7. He wasn't bad in the World Series, either, compiling a lifetime mark of 7-2.

For Ruffing, there were only two teams in the 1930s worth mentioning—the Yankees and Connie Mack's Philadelphia Athletics. "If it wasn't us, it was them." Aside from Rizzuto, who came to the Yankees in 1941, the only exceptions to that belief—Gehringer and Johnson—require no explanation for making it to his lineup. "Good is good."

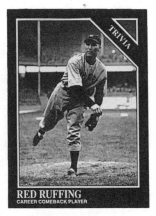

RED RUFFING
CAREER COMEBACK PLAYER

For Ruffing, there were only two teams in the 1930s worth mentioning—the Yankees and Connie Mack's Philadelphia Athletics. "If it wasn't us, it was them."

Career Highlights
Lifetime record: 273-225
Posted four 20-win seasons
Hall of Fame: 1967

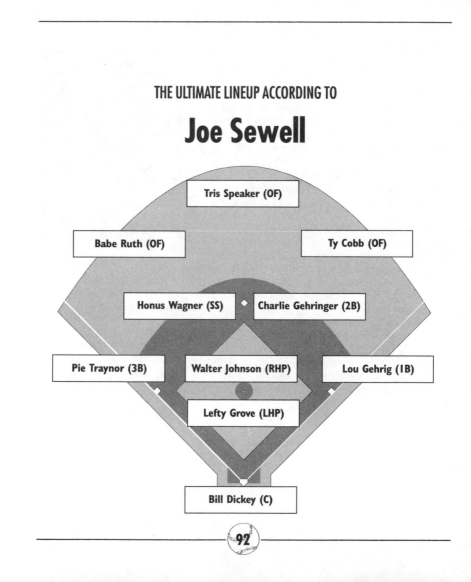

THE ULTIMATE LINEUP ACCORDING TO

Joe Sewell

Tris Speaker (OF)

Babe Ruth (OF)

Ty Cobb (OF)

Honus Wagner (SS)

Charlie Gehringer (2B)

Pie Traynor (3B)

Walter Johnson (RHP)

Lou Gehrig (1B)

Lefty Grove (LHP)

Bill Dickey (C)

THE GREATEST contact hitter in baseball history, Sewell was called up to play shortstop for the Indians after the fatal beaning of Ray Chapman in 1920. Over the next 14 years, he compiled a .312 average for Cleveland (1920-30) and the Yankees (1931-33), including a career-high of .353 in 1923.

The shortstop and third baseman holds just about all the records for fewest strikeouts, fanning only 114 times in 7,132 official at bats. Twice, he struck out only three times in a season; and in three other years he struck out only four times.

Walter Johnson and Lefty Grove aside, Sewell always considered Dutch Leonard his toughest mound opponent. "He was a spitballer with a good curve for the Red Sox and Tigers. And he was mean—he'd throw right at you if you crowded the plate, and sometimes even if you didn't."

Sewell's list of underrated players begins with his brother Luke, an American League catcher from 1921 to 1942. "He was a very smart player with the best arm around, although of course he never hit like Dickey. I'd also have to throw in outfielders Sammy West and Riggs Stephenson. You couldn't get a hit with West in center field; he'd grab everything that wasn't grounded through the infield. As for Stephenson, his .336 average should have gotten him into the Hall of Fame a long time ago."

JOE SEWELL
CLEVELAND INDIANS – SHORTSTOP   1922

Sewell always considered Dutch Leonard his toughest mound opponent.

Career Highlights
Lifetime batting average: .312
Struck out only 17 times over 462-game stretch, 1925-1927
Hall of Fame: 1977

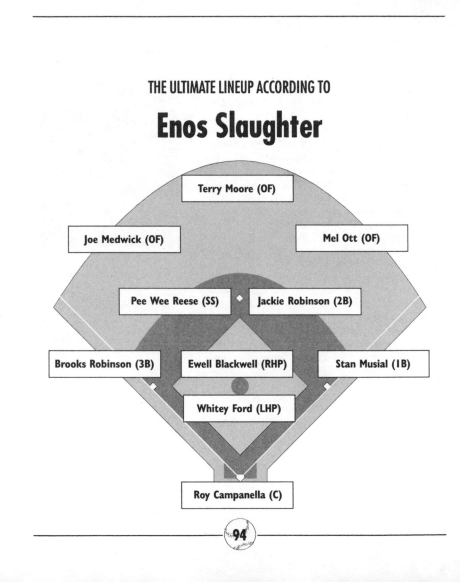

THE ULTIMATE LINEUP ACCORDING TO

Enos Slaughter

Terry Moore (OF)

Joe Medwick (OF)

Mel Ott (OF)

Pee Wee Reese (SS)

Jackie Robinson (2B)

Brooks Robinson (3B)

Ewell Blackwell (RHP)

Stan Musial (1B)

Whitey Ford (LHP)

Roy Campanella (C)

SLAUGHTER, A LEFTHAND-HITTING out-fielder, batted .300 in a 19-year career spent primarily with the Cardinals (1938-42, 1946-53), then later with the (1954-55), Athletics (1955-56), Yankees again (1956-59), and Braves (1959).

Slaughter's batting marks include National League-leading totals in doubles in 1939, in hits and triples in 1942, and in runs batted in 1946. He also scored exactly 100 runs in three different seasons.

While singling out teammate Moore as the most underrated player of his era, Slaughter would also make room somewhere on his roster for Brooklyn outfielder Pete Reiser, whose career was shortened by his mad dashes into walls. "I always thought Reiser was a much better outfielder for the Dodgers than Duke Snider or Carl Furillo. He never gave an inch, and I guess that was his undoing. Damn shame, those injuries of his."

His toughest pitcher? "That would have to be Carl Erskine of the Dodgers when he was at the top of his game. Most curveballers from the right side have trouble with lefties, but not him. He came right over the top, and that ball didn't take prisoners when he got it where he wanted it."

ENOS SLAUGHTER
ST. LOUIS CARDINALS – OUTFIELD   1938

Slaughter's fiery play made him synonymous with hustle, especially after a dramatic run from first base to home in the 1946 World Series that gave the Cardinals the championship over the Red Sox.

Career Highlights
Lifetime batting average: .300
Hall of Fame: 1985

THE ULTIMATE LINEUP ACCORDING TO
Duke Snider

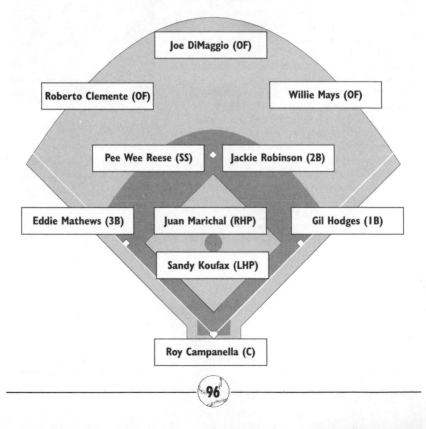

Joe DiMaggio (OF)

Roberto Clemente (OF)

Willie Mays (OF)

Pee Wee Reese (SS)

Jackie Robinson (2B)

Eddie Mathews (3B)

Juan Marichal (RHP)

Gil Hodges (1B)

Sandy Koufax (LHP)

Roy Campanella (C)

SNIDER WAS THE LEFTHANDED power on the Boys of Summer teams in Brooklyn that were otherwise heavily righthanded. The center fielder compiled a .295 average with 407 home runs for the Dodgers (1947-62), Mets (1963), and Giants (1964). He batted over .300 seven times, hit 40 or more home runs his last five seasons in Brooklyn, including a National League-leading 43 in 1956, and had six years of 100-plus runs batted in, leading the league with 136 in 1955.

Of his lineup, Snider says, "It isn't easy to leave Stan Musial out, but Gil Hodges has to be there for his glove and I'll take Joe DiMaggio over any other outfielder, *ever.*"

His mound choices are "no-brainers. Marichal had all the pitches. And Koufax, well, it was as if he were throwing imaginary fastballs. For myself, though, the most difficult pitcher was probably Bill Henry, the Cincinnati reliever. He was a lefty who threw nothing but fastballs. I could usually hit the fastball, but the harder he threw, the more I just popped up,"

The most underrated player was "without a doubt, Carl Furillo. He always did a great job defensively and offensively, including winning a batting crown, but he'd do it without notice. I suppose he just wasn't colorful enough for the press."

Comparing the Boys of Summer to the Big Red Machine of the 1970s, Snider says: "Sure, Cincinnati was great. But if you put the two teams together, Johnny Bench would have to play third and Pete Rose would have to play left. The rest of the Reds wouldn't break into the lineup."

Career Highlights
407 home runs
Hit 40 or more home runs five times
Hall of Fame: 1980

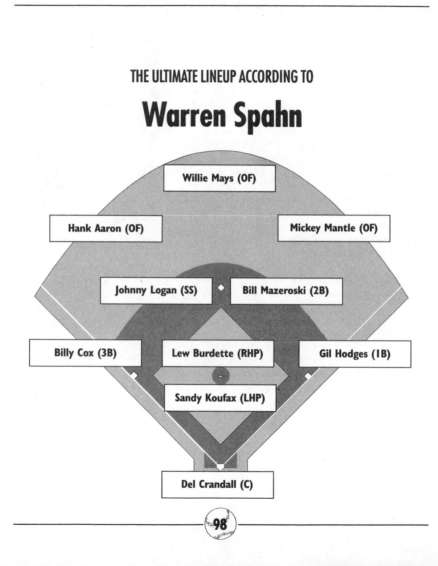

THE ULTIMATE LINEUP ACCORDING TO

Warren Spahn

Willie Mays (OF)

Hank Aaron (OF)

Mickey Mantle (OF)

Johnny Logan (SS)

Bill Mazeroski (2B)

Billy Cox (3B)

Lew Burdette (RHP)

Gil Hodges (1B)

Sandy Koufax (LHP)

Del Crandall (C)

THE MOST SUCCESSFUL southpaw in baseball history, with a mark of 363 wins against 245 losses and a 3.09 ERA, Spahn spent the first 20 years of his 21-year career with the Braves (1942, 1946-64), before splitting a final season between the Mets and Giants. He won 20 or more games 13 times to tie Christy Mathewson for the National League record.

Although Spahn won the Cy Young Award only once, in 1957 for a record of 21-11 and 2.69 ERA, he turned in even better performances in both 1953 (23-7, 2.10) and 1963 (23-7, 2.60). He also hurled two nohitters, the second coming in 1961 just days after he celebrated his fortieth birthday.

For Spahn, there aren't enough positions to accommodate the players he would like behind him for one game. "It really comes down to apples and oranges. Crandall, for instance, was a great lowball catcher on a lowball pitching team, so I would want him there from personal experience. But Johnny Bench had a better arm and a better bat. If I was thinking defense, I would have to have Hodges and Cox. But what about Stan Musial and Eddie Mathews for offense?"

He also dismisses the notion of one batter having been harder to handle than another. "Everybody who got up to the plate represented one-twenty-seventh of the problem."

Spahn led the National League in victories eight times, in ERA three times, in strikeouts four times, and in complete games nine times.

Career Highlights
Lifetime record: 363-245
Cy Young Award: 1957
Hall of Fame: 1973

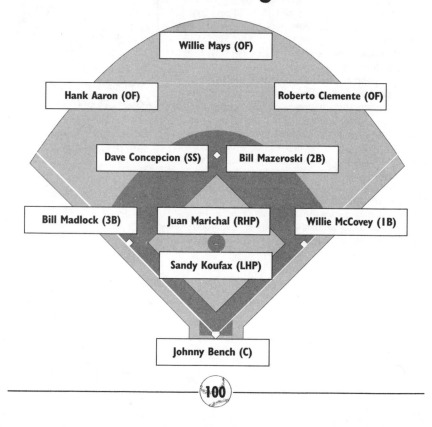

THE ULTIMATE LINEUP ACCORDING TO

Willie Stargell

Willie Mays (OF)

Hank Aaron (OF)

Roberto Clemente (OF)

Dave Concepcion (SS)

Bill Mazeroski (2B)

Bill Madlock (3B)

Juan Marichal (RHP)

Willie McCovey (1B)

Sandy Koufax (LHP)

Johnny Bench (C)

STARGELL REWROTE MOST of the statistical history of the Pittsburgh franchise when his 21 years with the Pirates (1962-82) produced 475 home runs, 953 extra-base hits, and 1,540 runs batted in. The lefty-hitting outfielder-first baseman ended up with a career average of .282 and numbered among his trophies home run crowns in both 1971 and 1973 and a shared Most Valuable Player award in 1979 (with Keith Hernandez). His most potent years at the plate were 1971 (.295, 48 homers, 125 runs batted in, and 104 runs scored) and 1973 (.299, 44 homers, 119 runs batted in, and 106 runs scored).

Stargell sees close calls at second and third, where Joe Morgan and Mike Schmidt rival Mazeroski and Madlock. He also proposes a backup outfield of Frank Robinson, Dale Murphy, and Dave Parker.

Although he also includes Joe and Phil Niekro, Ferguson Jenkins, and Don Sutton among the pitchers who bedeviled him the most, Stargell comes back to Marichal as his worst nemesis. "I'll never forget one game when he struck me out three times on three different pitches thrown three entirely different ways."

Madlock wins Stargell's endorsement as the most underrated player of his era. "The man won batting championships and was a great clutch hitter. He was also a leader in the clubhouse, although a lot of front office people never liked him because he always said what was on his mind. George Hendrick and Ron Cey were a couple of others who always seemed to slip between the cracks when media people got around to praising good players."

Although Stargell includes Joe and Phil Niekro, Ferguson Jenkins, and Don Sutton among the pitchers who bedeviled him the most, he comes back to Juan Marichal as his worst nemesis.

Career Highlights
475 home runs
1,540 runs batted in
Most Valuable Player: 1979
Hall of Fame: 1988

THE ULTIMATE LINEUP ACCORDING TO

Dazzy Vance

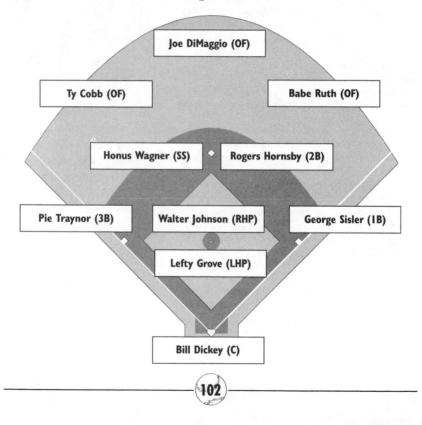

Joe DiMaggio (OF)

Ty Cobb (OF)

Babe Ruth (OF)

Honus Wagner (SS)

Rogers Hornsby (2B)

Pie Traynor (3B)

Walter Johnson (RHP)

George Sisler (1B)

Lefty Grove (LHP)

Bill Dickey (C)

RIGHTHANDER VANCE was the dominant strikeout artist of the 1920s and probably the finest pitcher in the history of the Brooklyn Dodgers. From the time he came up with the Pirates in 1915 until his retirement in 1935, he compiled a record of 197-140 with an ERA of 3.24 and a strikeout total of 2,045. Although he also hurled for the Yankees (1915, 1918), Cardinals (1933-34), and Reds (1934), in addition to the Pirates (1915), all but seven of his wins were registered in a Brooklyn uniform, which he wore between 1922 and 1932 and again in 1935.

A three-time 20-game winner, Vance also led the National League in ERA three times, in complete games twice, and in strikeouts for seven consecutive years (1922-28). In 1924, he won the National League's award as its Most Valuable Player on the basis of his 28-6 record, 2.16 ERA, and 262 strikeouts.

The curious thing about Vance's selections to his lineup is that they include only three National Leaguers—Hornsby, Traynor, and Wagner (who retired in 1917 when Vance had played in just one National League game). Only 10 of Vance's 442 major league mound appearances were in the junior circuit.

DAZZY VANCE
ST. LOUIS CARDINALS – PITCHER   1934

A three-time 20-game winner, Vance also led the National League in ERA three times, in complete games twice, and in strikeouts for seven consecutive years.

Career Highlights
Most Valuable Player: 1924
Hall of Fame: 1955

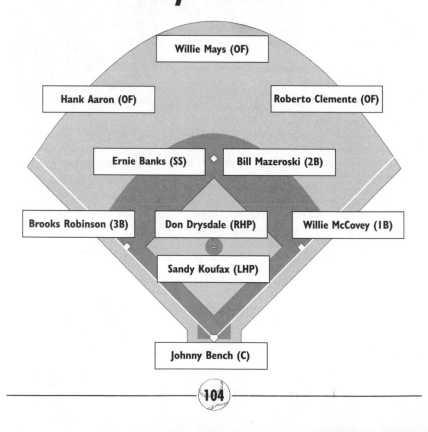

THE ULTIMATE LINEUP ACCORDING TO

Billy Williams

Willie Mays (OF)

Hank Aaron (OF)

Roberto Clemente (OF)

Ernie Banks (SS)

Bill Mazeroski (2B)

Brooks Robinson (3B)

Don Drysdale (RHP)

Willie McCovey (1B)

Sandy Koufax (LHP)

Johnny Bench (C)

FEW POWER HITTERS went as unnoticed as Williams did while he was batting .290 over an 18-year career with the Cubs (1959-74) and Athletics (1975-76). With most of the attention going to Chicago teammate Ernie Banks, the lefthand-hitting outfielder went about winning National League Rookie-of-the-Year honors in 1961, leading the senior circuit in hits and runs scored in 1970, setting the pace in batting and slugging averages in 1972, clouting at least 20 homers in 14 years, amassing 426 round-trippers in his career, and retiring with a then-National League record of 1,117 consecutive game appearances.

Williams had his most productive seasons in 1970 (.322, 42 home runs, 34 doubles, 129 runs batted in, and 137 runs scored) and 1972 (.333 batting average, .606 slugging percentage, 37 home runs, 34 doubles, and 122 runs batted in).

Williams's worst nightmare on the mound was southpaw Ray Sadecki, a journeyman southpaw who compiled a 135-131 record between 1960 and 1977. "It was really very simple. He knew he could get me out and I knew he could get me out, so he always got me out."

The most underrated player of his time? "Vada Pinson easily. He's always had the offensive numbers to be in the Hall of Fame—and that's without counting what a fine defensive player he was."

Williams's worst nightmare was journeyman southpaw Ray Sadecki.

Career Highlights

Lifetime batting average: .290

426 home runs

1,117 consecutive game appearances

Rookie of the Year: 1961

Hall of Fame: 1987

Addendum:
Hall of Famers
without Lineups

Bob Feller

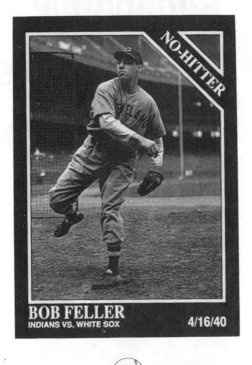

BOB FELLER
INDIANS VS. WHITE SOX   4/16/40

THE RIGHTHANDED FELLER spent his entire 18-year career with the Indians (1936-41, 1945-56), compiling a record of 266 wins against 162 losses and an ERA of 3.25. A fireballer with one of the best curves of his era, he won 20 or more games six times, leading or tying for the American League lead each time; topped all American League pitchers in strikeouts seven times; and hurled three no-hitters. His single best year was 1946, when he had a record of 26-15 with 36 complete games, 348 strikeouts, 10 shutouts, and an ERA of 2.18.

To pick the most underrated player of his time, Feller hops over to the National League to pick catcher Ernie Lombardi. "Anybody who could rack up .300 averages with the infielders playing in the outfield because he was so slow and could never beat out a hit, has to be a tremendous hitter. He deserved to be in the Hall of Fame years before he was finally elected there."

For Feller, the most troublesome hitters were "Tommy Henrich and Taft Wright from the left side, and Joe DiMaggio from the right. That was a personal thing, though. In an absolute sense, the greatest hitters I ever saw were Ted Williams and Rogers Hornsby. I didn't come out too badly with Williams, and Hornsby was essentially through as a player before I had to face him."

Career Highlights
Led league in victories six times
Lifetime ERA: 3.25
Threw 3 no-hitters
Hall of Fame: 1962

109

Rollie Fingers

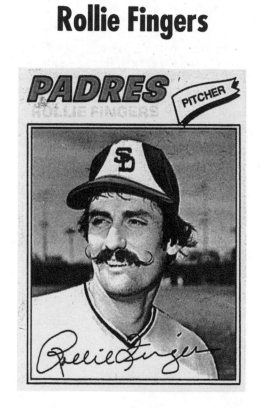

THE DOMINANT BULLPEN specialist of the 1970s and early 1980s, the righthanded Fingers was the first reliever to record 300 saves. He retired with a record 341 (since surpassed by Jeff Reardon and Lee Smith) after a 17-year career with the Athletics (1968-76), Padres (1977-80), and Brewers (1981-82, 1984-85). A won-lost record of 114-118 fails to reflect his lifetime ERA of 2.90.

Famous for his flamboyant handlebar moustache, Fingers led his league in saves three times; pitched in 70 or more games every year from 1974 to 1977, leading one league or the other in three of those seasons. He ranks fourth on the all-time list in mound appearances, with 944. The closer for the Oakland dynasty of the early 1970s, Fingers posted 7 saves, a 2-2 record, and a 1.35 ERA in his 16 appearances in three World Series.

If Fingers had to win one game, "I'd want Catfish Hunter on the mound. He had such great control and he always won the big one. I'd also want Robin Yount, George Brett, and Rod Carew in the lineup. Of course, I'd really want Ted Williams and Mickey Mantle. But I only watched them. I never had to pitch against them."

Frank Robinson, Harmon Killebrew, and Carew are the hitters who gave Fingers the most trouble. "Robinson hit everyone like he owned them, so maybe he doesn't count. Killebrew and Carew were as different as they could be. One was a power guy, the other a contact hitter, but both of them always seemed way too comfortable up there against me."

According to Fingers, "Underrated means Joe Rudi. He always got the clutch hit, always took the extra base, always made the spectacular play, but the A's just had too many big players with big personalities for anyone to notice him."

Career Highlights
341 saves
Cy Young Award: 1981
Most Valuable Player: 1981
Hall of Fame: 1992

Whitey Ford

ED "WHITEY" FORD

FORD WAS THE ACE of the Yankees for practically his entire 16-year career (1950, 1953-67). The southpaw's 236 victories and 106 losses with a 2.75 ERA, represents the highest won-lost percentage (.690) for pitchers with at least 200 wins. He led or tied for the lead in American League wins three times, in won-lost percentage three times, and in shutouts twice.

In 1961, Ford won the Cy Young Award for his 25-4 mark. He also holds World Series records for most Series played (11), most victories (10), most games (22), most strikeouts (94), and most consecutive scoreless innings (33 2/3).

Ford says that his most difficult hitters were Nellie Fox and Harvey Kuenn. "Fox would throw his bat, his head, or anything else at the ball to get one of those little dunkers between the infield and the outfield. Kuenn was like a scientist up there, always measuring you for disaster."

Fox and Kuenn aside, however, Ford also recalls one afternoon in 1956 at Griffith Stadium when Washington slugger Jim Lemon earned a special place in his memory as a foe. "Lemon was one of those guys who gave you strikeouts or home runs, and little in between. One afternoon we're playing the Senators in front of a packed house that included President Eisenhower. The first three times up, Lemon is boom, boom, boom—three home runs. In the ninth inning, though, we're still up 5-3, when he comes up again with a man on base. Casey Stengel comes out to the mound, and I wave him away. 'I can get this guy out,' I tell him. Casey pulls the ball out of my hand and says, 'Maybe, but I don't have another life to live to wait around for it.' In comes Tom Morgan from the bullpen, and he strikes out Lemon on three pitches."

Ford's .690 won-loss percentage (236-106) is the highest for pitchers with at least 200 wins.

Career Highlights
10 World Series wins
Cy Young Award: 1961
Hall of Fame: 1974

Bob Gibson

GIBSON WON 251 and lost 174 while compiling a 2.91 earned run average in 17 seasons with the Cardinals (1959-75). He won 20 or more games six times, leading the National League once in victories; struck out more than 200 batters nine times, leading the National League once; hurled 56 shutouts; and retired with 3,117 strikeouts. In 1968, he gave one of the most dominating pitching performances in the history of baseball, posting a record of 22-9 with 268 strikeouts, 13 shutouts, and a nearly invisible 1.12 ERA. In three World Series, he won 7 and lost only 2 while giving up only 1.89 runs every nine innings. During his career, the righthander collected two Cy Young Awards, picked up a Most Valuable Player trophy, fired a no-hitter, and gained a reputation as one of the game's fiercest competitors.

For Gibson, the toughest batters were "those banjo hitters at the top and bottom of the lineup who just slapped at the ball. None of them sticks out more than others. They were *all* annoying."

His choice of the most underrated player of his era falls on the lefty-swinging Al Oliver. "He was a consistent .300 hitter who seemed to get overlooked because his specialty was doubles instead of home runs. There was never an outfield gap that Al Oliver didn't like."

Gibson is widely considered to have had one of the most intimidating mound demeanors in baseball history.

Career Highlights
Lifetime record: 251-174
56 shutouts
3,117 strikeouts
Cy Young Award: 1968, 1970
Most Valuable Player: 1968
Hall of Fame: 1981

Reggie Jackson

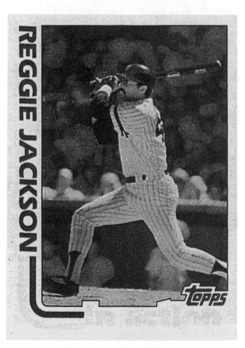

AS CONTROVERSIAL as he was productive, Jackson spent his 21-year career with the Athletics in Kansas City and Oakland (1967-75, 1987), Orioles (1976), Yankees (1977-81), and Angels (1982-86). The lefthand-hitting outfielder concluded his career with 563 home runs, the sixth highest total in history, and 2,597 strikeouts, far and away the all-time record.

Jackson led the American League twice each in runs scored and runs batted in, three times in slugging percentage, and four times in homers. He took Most Valuable Player honors in 1973 on the basis of his league leading totals in home runs (32), runs batted in (117), runs scored (99), and slugging percentage (.531) to go along with a .293 batting average.

Jackson put up even more imposing numbers in 1969—.275, 47 homers, 118 runs batted in, and league-leading totals of 123 runs scored and .608 in slugging. Dubbed "Mr. October" for his postseason heroics, Jackson played in 45 games in 11 League Championship Series, both records, and in five World Series. His overall slugging average of .755 is a World Series high, and in the 1977 classic he set new standards with a 1.250 slugging percentage and five home runs, three of them in the same game, on consecutive pitches, off three different Dodger pitchers.

Asked which pitcher was most difficult for him, Jackson replies: "I did very little against two lefties, Mike Caldwell and Scott McGregor, for a few years anyway. Eventually, I caught up with both of them, though. It was really Jim Palmer who stands out in this context; I had some success against him overall, but he was so good in clutch situations that I never really hurt him when the game was on the line."

Asked which pitcher was most difficult for him, Jackson singles out Jim Palmer.

Career Highlights
563 home runs
Most Valuable Player: 1973
Hall of Fame: 1993

Judy Johnson

WILLIAM JULIUS JOHNSON
"JUDY"
NEGRO LEAGUES 1923-1937

CONSIDERED BEST THIRD BASEMAN OF HIS
DAY IN NEGRO LEAGUES. OUTSTANDING AS
FIELDER AND EXCELLENT CLUTCH HITTER
WHO BATTED OVER .300 MOST OF CAREER.
HELPED HILLDALE TEAM WIN THREE FLAGS
IN ROW, 1923-24-25. ALSO PLAYED FOR
1935 CHAMPION PITTSBURGH CRAWFORDS.

THE FOREMOST THIRD BASEMAN of the Negro Leagues, the righthand-hitting Johnson played 16 seasons (1921-36) for the Darby Hilldale Club, Homestead Grays, Darby Daisies, and Pittsburgh Crawfords. A lifetime .300 hitter who topped the .400 mark in 1929, Johnson appeared in three Negro World Series.

Johnson claims: "There were too many great players to pick just one team. But I will tell you that Josh Gibson was the best hitter I've ever seen. I signed him for the Grays in 1930 when he was just a teenager, and later on we played together on the Crawfords. Cool Papa Bell and Oscar Charleston were on the Crawfords with us too. It was the best team I ever saw, maybe the best ever, black or white."

In a game that had to be won, Johnson would put one of two pitchers on the mound: "Satchel Paige or Dizzy Dean. They went up against each other lots of times in exhibition games and barnstorming tours, and Satch won more than he lost. But I could live with either of them."

"Josh Gibson was the best hitter I've ever seen."

Career Highlights
Lifetime .300 hitter
Hall of Fame: 1975

Mickey Mantle

MANTLE BATTED .298 with 536 home runs (eighth on the all-time list) and 1,509 runs batted in over his 18-year (1951-68) career with the Yankees, most of it spent as a center fielder. The switch-hitting slugger, who was also considered one of the fastest men in baseball in the 1950s, led the junior circuit in batting and runs batted in once, in slugging percentage three times, and in home runs four times.

Mantle's personal highs were a .365 average in 1957 and 54 homers in 1962. A three-time Most Valuable Player (1956, 1957, 1962), Mantle won the Triple Crown in 1956 by batting .353 with 52 home runs and 130 runs batted in. In 12 World Series, he established records for most home runs (18), runs batted in (40), runs scored (42), and walks (43).

Mantle says about selecting a lineup: "If we were choosing sides and every player was in the pool, my first pick would be Whitey Ford and my second would be Ted Williams. Beyond that there would be just too many and I'd be afraid of leaving somebody out. Besides, with Whitey on the mound and Williams in the lineup, the rest of the team wouldn't much matter; we'd still beat just about anybody."

The toughest pitcher? "That would be Sandy Koufax, even though he was in the National League and I didn't have to face him very much. Among American League lefties I'd have to pick Herb Score before he got hurt. From the right side, no question: Dick Radatz of the Red Sox. I once read in a Dallas newspaper that I faced Radatz 66 times in my career and that he struck me out 45 times. If he wasn't the toughest, I don't want to remember who was."

"The most underrated guy is the one who will do absolutely anything to win a game. The two who come to mind immediately are Billy Martin and Pete Rose."

Career Highlights
536 home runs
1,509 runs batted in
Most Valuable Player Awards: 1956, 1957, 1962
Triple Crown: 1956
Hall of Fame: 1974

Eddie Mathews

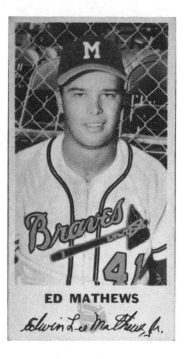

ED MATHEWS

SECOND ONLY TO Mike Schmidt as the game's greatest slugging third baseman, Mathews bashed 512 home runs in a 17-year career for the Braves in Boston, Milwaukee, and Atlanta (1952-66), then later for the Astros (1967) and Tigers (1967-68). The lefty-swinger led the National League in home runs twice, hit at least 40 in four seasons, scored more than 100 runs eight times, and drove in more than 100 five times.

For most of his career with the Braves, Mathews teamed with Hank Aaron for the most potent one-two longball punch in baseball history, surpassing even the home run marks of such tandems as Babe Ruth and Lou Gehrig, and Willie Mays and Willie McCovey.

The most underrated player of his era? "Let's put it this way: I hit more than 500 home runs and I'm in the Hall of Fame, so why doesn't American Express want me to do commercials for them? And another thing: Ernie Banks and I ended up with exactly the same number of home runs, but it took me almost five years more to get into Cooperstown. Nothing against Ernie, but I even look better in a lobby."

Mathews' toughest pitcher, he contends, was Juan Marichal. "Without question. He usually got me out. That's why I felt even better when he happened to be the guy who served up my 500th home run."

Career Highlights
512 home runs
1,453 runs batted in
Hall of Fame: 1978

Robin Roberts

ONE OF BASEBALL'S midcentury workhorses, Roberts won 286 and lost 245 in 19 seasons with the Phillies (1948-61), Orioles (1962-65), Astros (1965-66), and Cubs (1966). The righthander won at least 20 games for six consecutive seasons between 1950 and 1955, topping the National League in victories for four of those seasons and reaching a career-high 28 triumphs in 1952.

For six straight seasons Roberts led the National League in games started, for five straight in innings pitched and complete games, and twice in strikeouts and shutouts. The classic "smart" pitcher, he yielded more home runs than any other hurler almost annually, but they were almost always solo shots that didn't endanger his lead. As a union representative, he was instrumental in bringing in Marvin Miller as the head of the Players Association.

Roberts's toughest adversary was Ernie Banks. "He hit about 15 home runs against me in key situations, and pitching against him in Wrigley Field was something I could have done without. But I would have to say that the worst blow of my career was when Joe DiMaggio hit a home run off me in the tenth inning of a 1950 World Series game to give the Yankees a 2-1 win. That was my only World Series appearance and that pitch was the one that, of all the thousands I threw, I've regretted the most."

"The most underrated player would have to be Del Ennis. He was a solid, productive hitter for the Phillies, but he was from Philadelphia and the fans used to really give it to him. It can be hard sometimes to be recognized in your own town."

Career Highlights
Lifetime record: 286-245
Led league in victories 4 times
Six 20-win seasons
Hall of Fame: 1976

Frank Robinson

FRANK ROBINSON
CINCINNATI REDS   1st BASE-OUTFIELD

THE ONLY PLAYER TO WIN a Most Valuable Player award in each league, Robinson spent his 21 major league seasons with the Reds (1956-65), Orioles (1966-71), Angels (1972-74), and Indians (1974-76). The righthanded outfielder ranks fourth on the all-time home run list with 586. His National League Most Valuable Player award came in 1961, when he batted .323 with 37 homers, 124 runs batted in, 117 runs scored, and a league leading .611 slugging average.

Robinson's American League trophy came in his first year in Baltimore, after Cincinnati let him get away in one of the worst trades in history; that year he won the Triple Crown (.316, 49, 122), and led the American League in runs (122) and slugging (.637). The .294 career hitter's numbers were equally impressive in 1962, when he reached personal highs in batting (.342), runs batted in (136), and runs scored (134), and notched another of his four slugging crowns. He was also National League Rookie of the Year in 1956. Robinson became the first black manager in the major leagues when he took over the reins at Cleveland in 1975. Later, he also managed the Giants and Orioles.

His greatest mound nemesis? "You won't get any surprise answers from me. Don Drysdale, for all the obvious reasons. Before he'd let you get a hit off him, he'd hit you."

As the pitcher to start one must-win game, "I'm torn between Sandy Koufax and Bob Gibson. I wouldn't be embarrassed sending either of them out there for the seventh game of the World Series. But, then again, if they were both on my pitching staff, the Series would never get to the seventh game, would it?"

Most underrated player of his time? "Tony Perez. In the bottom of the ninth with the winning run on second and two out, I'd want Tony at the plate. He always did what had to be done in clutch situations."

Career Highlights
586 home runs
1,812 runs batted in
Rookie of the Year: 1956
Most Valuable Player: 1961, 1966
Triple Crown: 1966
Hall of Fame: 1982

Edd Roush

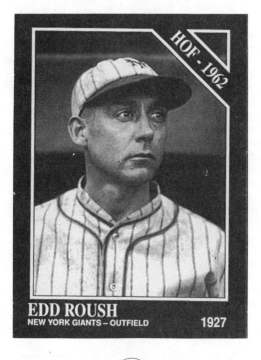

EDD ROUSH
NEW YORK GIANTS – OUTFIELD   1927

HOF · 1962

ROUSH HAD AN 18-year career with the White Sox (1913), the Federal League franchises in Indianapolis (1914) and Newark (1915), the Giants (1916, 1927-29), and the Reds (1916-26, 1931). A left-handed hitter with a lifetime mark of .323, he led the National League in batting twice, and in slugging percentage, doubles, and triples once. He had 13 seasons with averages higher than .300 and was regarded as the premier defensive center fielder of his day. As assertive in his dealings with owners and general managers as he was with opponents on the field, Roush held out several times, most prominently in 1930 when he sat out the entire season in protest over a salary cut.

He names two teammates with the Reds as underrated players. "I'll take Jake Daubert. The man won batting championships, in 1913 and 1914, but you'd never know it. As far as I am concerned, he belongs in the Hall of Fame ahead of a lot of others in there today. Same thing with Heinie Groh. Daubert and Groh, they went out on the field to play, not like some of these modern players who walk out there, dig a hole in the batter's box, get in to hit, call time to dig another hole, then take a pitch, then dig some more. Seems like a lot more hole digging than baseball playing going on these days."

Roush's view of opposing players was egalitarian and simple. "I don't know who was tough and who was easy. They were all about the same to me, and they knew that, too. They all knew that if they got in my way, they got hurt."

Career Highlights
Lifetime batting average: .323
Hall of Fame: 1962

Red Schoendienst

SCHOENDIENST WAS A switch-hitting second baseman for the Cardinals (1945-56, 1961-63), Giants (1956-57), and Braves (1957-60). Before tuberculosis put the brakes on his career, he had been considered one of the National League's premier contact hitters from the leadoff or second spot in the batting order, and in that role helped push St. Louis to a flag in 1946 and Milwaukee to a couple of pennants ten years later. His best offensive year was 1953 when he batted .342.

Schoendienst also led the National League in stolen bases in his rookie season and in doubles in 1950. He ended up with a career mark of .289, despite spending five seasons battling his illness. Between his playing days and serving as team manager from 1965 to 1976 and parts of two other seasons, as well as an ongoing coaching job, Schoendienst has worn the St. Louis uniform longer than anyone else in the history of the franchise.

For Schoendienst, the toughest pitchers were Carl Erskine and Johnny Podres from the Boys of Summer teams in Brooklyn. "Erskine had an overhand curve and Podres a great changeup, but they were alike in hiding the ball. Those are personal choices, though. If you had to send someone out to the mound to win a single game, you wouldn't want anyone but Bob Gibson."

The most underrated player of his time? "Two Cardinal infielders—Whitey Kurowski and Dal Maxvill. Maxvill, especially, wasn't much with a bat, but nobody has ever played shortstop better."

Career Highlights
Lifetime batting average: .289
Hall of Fame: 1989

Tom Seaver

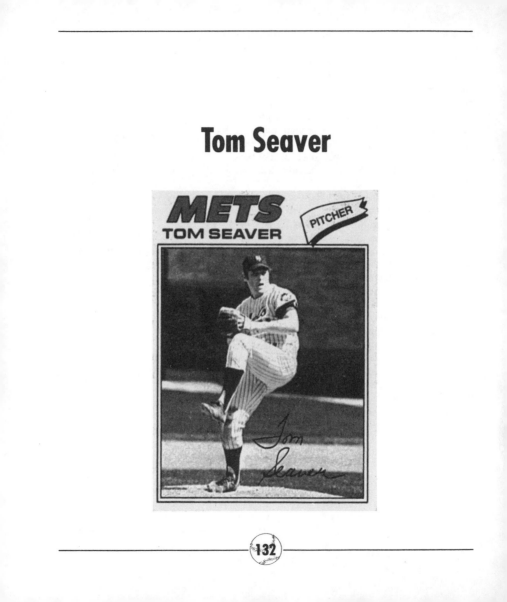

THE RIGHTHANDED SEAVER compiled a 311-205 record and a 2.86 ERA in a career that spanned two decades for the Mets (1967-77, 1983), Reds (1977-82), White Sox (1984-86), and Red Sox (1986). He also recorded 61 shutouts and 3,640 strikeouts, including a major league-record nine consecutive seasons (1968-76) of more than 200. (He added a tenth 200-plus season in 1978 to establish a National League mark.) The 1967 Rookie of the Year, Seaver quickly became The Franchise for the Mets, earning three Cy Young Awards in 1969 (25-7, 2.21 ERA), 1973 (19-10, 2.08), and 1975 (22-9, 2.38).

Overall, Seaver chalked up five seasons with 20 or more victories, topping all pitchers in his league in that category three times. He also set the pace in strikeouts five times, won-lost percentage four times, and ERA three times. On April 20, 1970, he tied a National League record by striking out 19, concluding the game by fanning the last 10 batters to establish a major league record for most K's in a row.

Seaver on his dream lineup: "You take the first pick and I'll take the second and we'll come up even. For instance, if you say Mickey Mantle, I'll say Willie Mays; if you say Henry Aaron, I'll say Roberto Clemente. When you're competing at that level of ability, the margins of difference aren't that great. Besides, the choices will vary from day to day, depending on emotion and recollection."

There is no hesitation on Seaver's part to dispel the impression that Tommy Hutton was his chief antagonist. "I had a lot more difficulty with the big, lefthanded power hitters. More probably than Hutton, it was Willie Stargell or Willie McCovey who hurt me the most."

Career Highlights
311 wins
61 shutouts
3,640 strikeouts
Rookie of the Year: 1967
Cy Young Award: 1969, 1973, 1975
Hall of Fame: 1992

Bill Terry

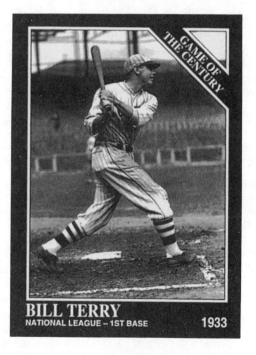

BILL TERRY
NATIONAL LEAGUE – 1ST BASE
1933

TERRY BATTED A LOFTY .341 in 14 years with the New York Giants (1923-36). The left-hand-hitting first baseman's mark of .401 in 1930 represented the last time a National Leaguer reached the .400 level. To reach that average, he knocked out 254 base hits, tying the National League record for safeties in a single season. Aside from base hits and batting average, the only category in which he posted league leading totals was triples, in 1931. He also managed the Giants to three pennants during a 10-year run as the New York pilot (1932-41).

"The most underrated player in my mind was me. It took them almost 20 years to elect me to the Hall of Fame, and the reason for that was that I wasn't too well liked by all those newspapermen who decide such things. Then again, you have to wonder about the players they elect there anyway. A lot of them were just good at one thing—hitting, fielding, or running. I always thought you had to be a great player all-around."

"The most underrated player in my mind was me. It took them almost 20 years to elect me to the Hall of Fame, and the reason for that was that I wasn't too well liked by all those newspapermen who decide such things."

Career Highlights
Lifetime batting average: .341
Hall of Fame: 1954

Ted Williams

ONE OF THE MOST potent hitters in baseball history, the lefty-swinging Williams batted .344 with 521 home runs in 19 seasons (between 1939 and 1960) for the Red Sox. The last major leaguer to reach .400 (.406 in 1941), the outfielder topped the American League in important offensive categories no less than 39 times, including batting six times, home runs four times, runs batted in four times, slugging average nine times, runs scored six times, and walks eight times.

Williams won the Triple Crown in 1942 (.356, 36, 137) and 1947 (.343, 32, 114). He was chosen Most Valuable Player in 1946 and 1949. Impressive as they are, Williams's numbers might have been even more imposing if he had not lost significant time to military service in both World War II and the Korean War.

His toughest pitcher was "also the greatest I ever saw—Bob Feller. But I think I'd also have to give an honorable mention to Bob Lemon, Whitey Ford, and Hoyt Wilhelm for the combination of their delivery and the liveliness of their ball. Eddie Joost, the shortstop for the Athletics, was the most underrated player of my time. He was the backbone of that team for about three or four years."

The last major leaguer to bat .400.

Career Highlights
.344 batting average
521 home runs
2,019 walks
1,839 runs batted in
Triple Crown: 1942, 1947
Most Valuable Player: 1946, 1949
Hall of Fame: 1966

Early Wynn

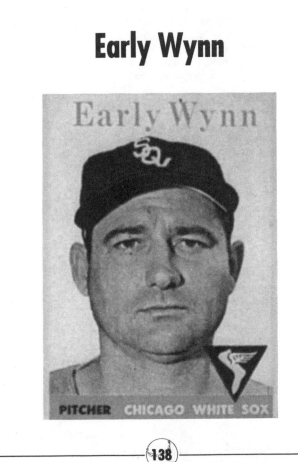

RIGHTHANDER WYNN POSTED a 300-244 record with a 3.54 ERA in a 23-year career with the Senators (1939, 1941-44, 1946-48), Indians (1949-57, 1963), and White Sox (1958-62). His greatest seasons—including five years of winning 20 or more games, two strikeout titles, and one ERA crown—came during his stays with Cleveland and Chicago. In both 1954 and 1959, he was the workhorse for pennant-winning teams, in the latter year copping a Cy Young Award for the White Sox.

Asked about notching his 300th win, Wynn explains: "The 300th win became important to me once I'd reached 200. I was going to get that 300th win no matter what it took. My manager at Cleveland at the time, Birdie Tebbetts, said I was crazy. He said I would've been better off winning 299 games because nobody had ever done that before and I would've become even more famous for failing than succeeding. But that wasn't how I saw it, and I'm just grateful for the patience that allowed me to get it finally."

Wynn's toughest batter was Yogi Berra. "He hit everything I threw, including one time I bounced a curve six feet in front of the plate and he slammed it for a double."

Career Highlights
300 wins
Cy Young Award: 1959
Won 20 or more games five times
Hall of Fame: 1972

Addendum:
Threshold Hall of
Famer Teams

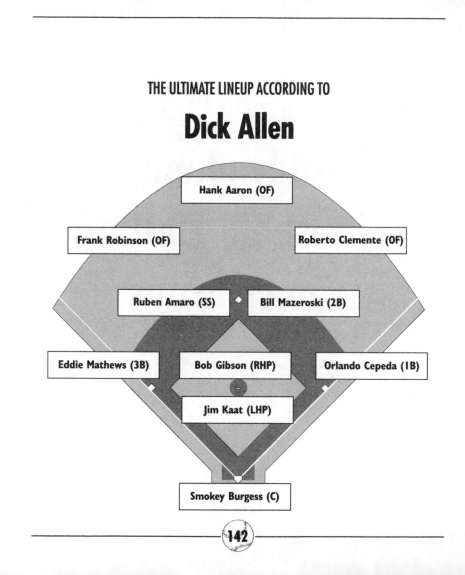

THE ULTIMATE LINEUP ACCORDING TO

Dick Allen

Hank Aaron (OF)

Frank Robinson (OF)

Roberto Clemente (OF)

Ruben Amaro (SS)

Bill Mazeroski (2B)

Eddie Mathews (3B)

Bob Gibson (RHP)

Orlando Cepeda (1B)

Jim Kaat (LHP)

Smokey Burgess (C)

SLUGGER ALLEN SPREAD his 15-year career over stints with the Phillies (1963-69, 1975-76), Cardinals (1970), Dodgers (1971), White Sox (1972-74), and Athletics (1977). The righthanded hitter moved back and forth between first base, third base, and the outfield; he batted over .300 six times (.292 lifetime) and clouted at least 30 home runs in the same number of seasons (351 lifetime).

Allen's best year was 1972, when he took American League Most Valuable Player honors for pacing the circuit in homers, runs batted in, slugging percentage, and walks, while averaging .308. He also led the American League in home runs in 1972.

For Allen, there were three tough calls in selecting his lineup: "Nobody was a better first baseman than Bill White, and he was a hard out. But I think Cepeda was awesome offensively. Mike Schmidt hit more home runs and Brooks Robinson had a better glove, but Mathews was just so good in so many ways. And I know Sandy Koufax was overpowering, but Kaat could beat you with his bat or his glove as well as on the mound."

When asked who was the most underrated player of his era, Allen points to Hank Aaron. "He had all those offensive stats, but he could also beat you with his glove or steal a base when the game was on the line."

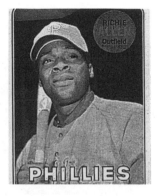

Allen has no doubts who his toughest pitcher was: "Number 45! Everything about Bob Gibson was tough. He was the total pitcher. He got you out not only with his pitching but also with his fielding and his competitive attitude."

Career Highlights
351 home runs
Rookie of the Year: 1964
Most Valuable Player: 1972

THE ULTIMATE LINEUP ACCORDING TO
Richie Ashburn

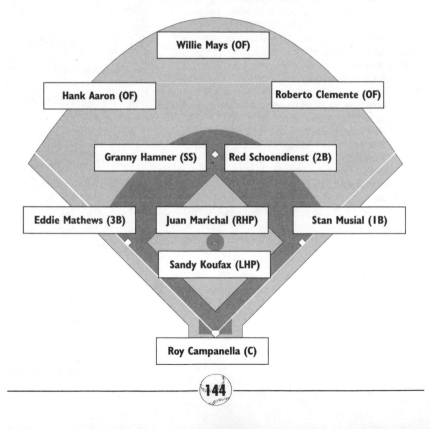

Willie Mays (OF)

Hank Aaron (OF)

Roberto Clemente (OF)

Granny Hamner (SS)

Red Schoendienst (2B)

Eddie Mathews (3B)

Juan Marichal (RHP)

Stan Musial (1B)

Sandy Koufax (LHP)

Roy Campanella (C)

A PREMIER LEADOFF HITTER of the 1950s, center fielder Ashburn batted .308 playing for the Phillies (1948-59), Cubs (1960-61), and Mets (1962). The speedy lefty swinger led the National League in walks four times, in hits three times, in triples twice, and in batting twice (.338 in 1955 and .350 in 1958). Ashburn was also a superb defensive player. Only eight times has an outfielder had as many as 500 putouts in one season, and he did it four times.

Ashburn's toughest pitcher was Sal Maglie. "He wasn't overpowering, but his pitches were hard for me to identify. They came in to you like fastballs, but then they broke an inch or two at the plate."

According to Ashburn, the most underrated player of his time was a teammate in Philadelphia. "Del Ennis has better stats than some people in the Hall of Fame." In fact, the righty-hitting left fielder drove in more than 100 runs per season seven times during his 14-year career with the Phillies, Cardinals, Reds, and White Sox, averaging .284 with 288 home runs.

RICHIE ASHBURN
OUTFIELD · PHILADELPHIA PHILLIES

Ashburn's one quibble about his ideal lineup is at shortstop. "I took Granny Hamner for all-around play even though Roy McMillan from Cincinnati was a better fielder. But if you let me take Duke Snider there, I'll choose him instead of either Hamner or McMillan."

Career Highlights
Lifetime batting average: .308
Led league in hits three times

THE ULTIMATE LINEUP ACCORDING TO

Bobby Bonds

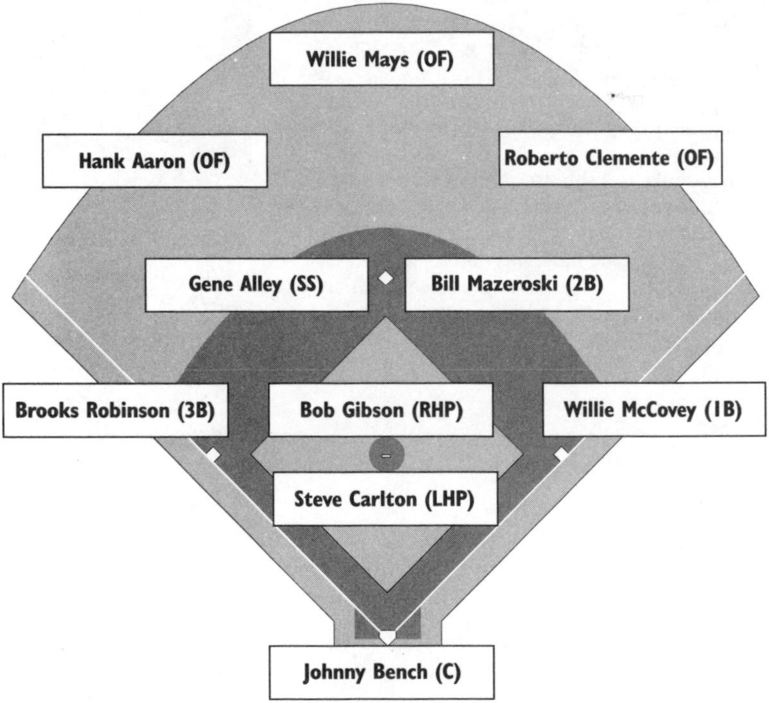

Willie Mays (OF)

Hank Aaron (OF)

Roberto Clemente (OF)

Gene Alley (SS)

Bill Mazeroski (2B)

Brooks Robinson (3B)

Bob Gibson (RHP)

Willie McCovey (1B)

Steve Carlton (LHP)

Johnny Bench (C)

BONDS HAD 30 HOME RUNS and 30 stolen bases in the same season five times. Over 14 big league seasons with the Giants (1968-74), Yankees (1975), Angels (1976-77), White Sox (1978), Rangers (1978), Indians (1979), Cardinals (1980), and Cubs (1981), the righthand-hitting outfielder batted .268, clouted 332 home runs, and swiped 461 bases. He hit more than 25 homers nine times, batted in more than 100 runs twice, stole a minimum of 40 bases seven times, and won three Gold Glove Awards.

Bonds insists on several honorable mentions to his lineup, especially at third base. "Eddie Mathews and Ken Boyer didn't have Robinson's glove, but they were great hitters. Jim Davenport should also be remembered because he was such a great clutch hitter. Bench was Bench, one of the greatest catchers who ever played the game, but as a baserunner I feared Jerry Grote of the Mets the most. He always threw the ball on the base. The infielders never had to tag you, you just slid into your own out. No apologies for Gene Alley; he and Maz turned the double play better and more often than any other pair. I'd like to make room for Ernie Banks, but he'll have to settle for an honorable mention at first."

Bonds' toughest pitcher was Andy Messersmith. "He had the best changeup I've ever seen. The remarkable thing is that he delivered it with exactly the same arm speed as his fastball."

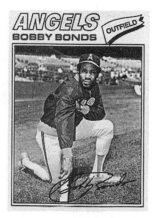

ANGELS
BOBBY BONDS
OUTFIELD

Bonds says that the most underrated player of his time is "Jim Gantner of the Brewers. He could beat you in a dozen ways that never showed up in statistics."

Career Highlights
332 home runs
461 stolen bases

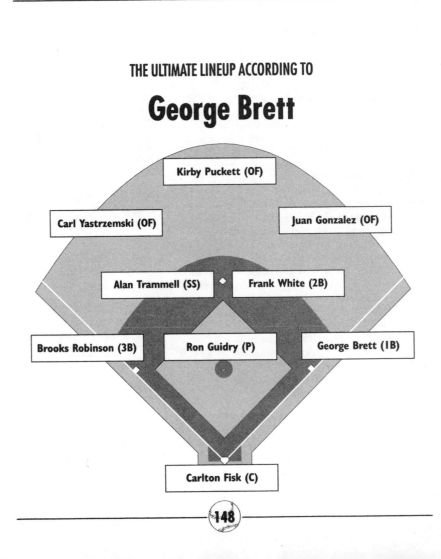

THE ULTIMATE LINEUP ACCORDING TO

George Brett

Kirby Puckett (OF)

Carl Yastrzemski (OF)

Juan Gonzalez (OF)

Alan Trammell (SS)

Frank White (2B)

Brooks Robinson (3B)

Ron Guidry (P)

George Brett (1B)

Carlton Fisk (C)

THE FRANCHISE PLAYER for the Kansas City Royals, with whom he spent his entire 21-year (1973-93) career, Brett collected 3,154 hits toward a .305 lifetime batting average. The lefty-batting third and first baseman also hit 317 home runs, and led the American League in doubles once and in hits and triples three times each. His career year came in 1980 when he took Most Valuable Player honors for leading the American League in batting with a .390 average, clouting 24 homers, and knocking in 118 runs.

Between May 8 and May 19, 1976, Brett established a major league record by stroking three or more hits in six straight games. In six League Championship Series (LCS), he also established records for highest slugging percentage (.728), runs scored (22), triples (4), and home runs (9). His three homers against the Yankees on October 6, 1978, were the big blows in his setting the single LCS record for slugging percentage (1.056).

Brett says of his lineup: "I put myself at first because there was no one like Brooks Robinson at third. Gonzalez is there because he is the next dominant player in the game. And, if you can have the Ron Guidry of 1978, when he won all those games, you don't need another pitcher."

Teammate Frank White gets Brett's nod as the most underrated player of his time: "I watched him every day for 15 years, and I don't think there has ever been a second baseman who could do the things he did. And he could hit, too."

Between May 8 and May 19, 1976, Brett established a major league record by stroking three or more hits in six straight games.

Career Highlights
3,154 hits
317 home runs
Most Valuable Player: 1980

149

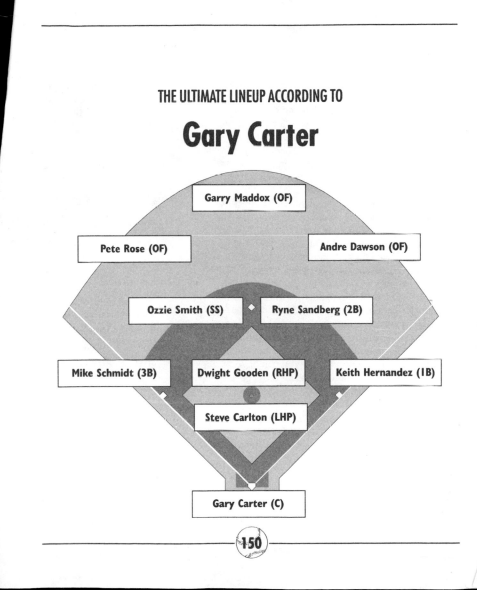

THE ULTIMATE LINEUP ACCORDING TO

Gary Carter

Garry Maddox (OF)

Pete Rose (OF)

Andre Dawson (OF)

Ozzie Smith (SS)

Ryne Sandberg (2B)

Mike Schmidt (3B)

Dwight Gooden (RHP)

Keith Hernandez (1B)

Steve Carlton (LHP)

Gary Carter (C)

CARTER SPENT 18 SEASONS behind the plate for the Expos (1974-84, 1992), Mets (1985-89), Giants (1990), and Dodgers (1991). A superlative defensive receiver with longball power, the righty-swinging Carter holds the National League record for catching the most games, over the course of which he batted .262 with 324 home runs.

Carter's best seasons were 1984, when he batted .294 with 27 homers and a league-leading 106 runs batted in, and the following season, when his numbers were .281, 32, and 100. He also had two other seasons with more than 100 runs batted in and eight more with 20 or more homers.

Carter's batting order for his lineup: "Rose would lead off, followed by Sandberg. Hernandez, Schmidt, and Dawson would be the heart of the order. With all due respect to Johnny Bench, I would catch and bat sixth. Maddox would bat seventh— but he's really there because nobody was better at running down fly balls—and Smith eighth."

Carter says about tough pitchers: "My concentration was always better against the truly great pitchers, so I rose to the occasion when I faced them. It was Don Robinson who consistently gave me the most trouble all those years he was with Pittsburgh. Then he was traded to the Giants in his last year and I finally got to him—probably to the tune of .200 or so."

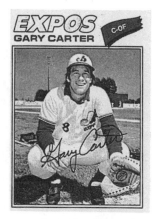

According to Carter, the most underrated player of his time was Andre Dawson "because he was in Montreal, and not one of the big media markets, for so long."

Career Highlights
2,056 games caught
324 home runs

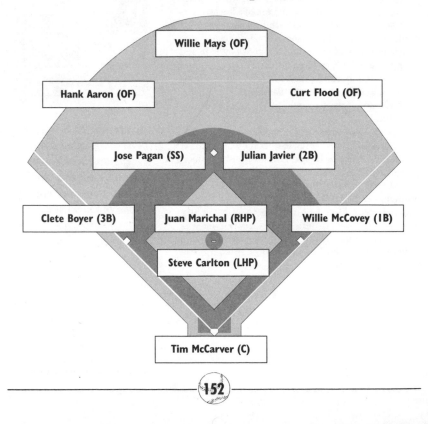

THE ULTIMATE LINEUP ACCORDING TO

Orlando Cepeda

Willie Mays (OF)

Hank Aaron (OF)

Curt Flood (OF)

Jose Pagan (SS)

Julian Javier (2B)

Clete Boyer (3B)

Juan Marichal (RHP)

Willie McCovey (1B)

Steve Carlton (LHP)

Tim McCarver (C)

FROM HIS ROOKIE-OF-THE-YEAR debut with the Giants in 1958, the righthand-hitting first baseman went on to become one of the National League's prominent power hitters for most of his career, winding up with a .297 average that included 379 home runs.

After leaving San Francisco in 1966 in an unpopular trade, Cepeda went on to productive seasons with the Cardinals (1966-68) and Braves (1969-72) before winding down in the American League with the Athletics (1972), Red Sox (1973), and Royals (1974). Cepeda led the National League in doubles in 1958, home runs in 1961, and runs batted in in 1961 and 1967. In 1967, his .325 average, 25 home runs, and 111 runs batted in won him Most Valuable Player recognition.

Flood is a particularly ardent choice to his lineup. "He was overlooked throughout his career, even though he was one of the best defensive center fielders of any era. People also forget that Flood's patience and knowledge of the strike zone allowed Lou Brock, who batted ahead of him, to steal all those bases. Billy Williams was another player who was overshadowed. In Chicago, Ernie Banks was so popular that *everybody* else was overshadowed.

Javier and Pagan were defensive specialists, although Javier also batted in the .280s twice and hit as many as 14 home runs, and Pagan became an excellent pinch hitter.

Cepeda chooses Hall of Famers Don Drysdale and Ferguson Jenkins as his most formidable mound opponents. "You never got comfortable with either of them, and if you made the mistake of even looking comfortable, you paid for it."

Career Highlights
Lifetime batting average: .297
379 home runs
Most Valuable Player: 1967

153

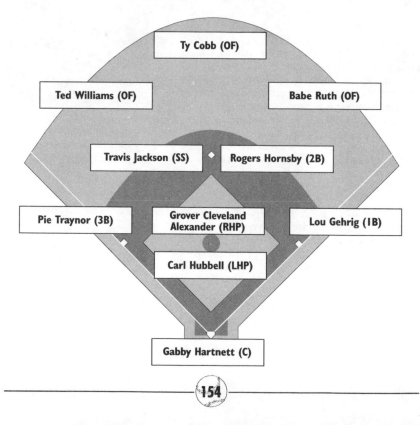

THE ULTIMATE LINEUP ACCORDING TO

Babe Herman

Ty Cobb (OF)

Ted Williams (OF)

Babe Ruth (OF)

Travis Jackson (SS)

Rogers Hornsby (2B)

Pie Traynor (3B)

Grover Cleveland Alexander (RHP)

Lou Gehrig (1B)

Carl Hubbell (LHP)

Gabby Hartnett (C)

HERMAN WAS ONE of the National League's most feared hitters over a 13-year career that started in Brooklyn in 1926 and ended in Ebbets Field 20 years later, when he returned for a brief wartime appearance. In between the Dodger years, he played for the Reds (1932), Cubs (1933-34), Pirates (1935), Reds again (1935-36), and Tigers (1937), coming out with a career average of .324 and 181 home runs. His nine .300-plus seasons included marks of .381 in 1929 and .393 in 1930. In the latter year, he also crushed 35 homers and 48 doubles, and drove home 130 runs. In 1932, he led the National League in triples.

His toughest pitcher was Bill Hallahan. "He was always wild enough to keep me off balance at the plate."

The most underrated player of his time? "Johnny Frederick. Before he broke his leg and became known as a pinch hitter, he was the best outfielder I played with. I always knew where he was. We lost the pennant in 1930 because he got hurt. I should also mention Bullet Joe Rogan of the Kansas City Monarchs. He was faster than Satchel Paige, better than anyone else in the Negro Leagues, as good as anyone in the majors. And he hit so well that he played the outfield when he wasn't on the mound—and batted cleanup sometimes even when he was pitching."

BABE HERMAN
CATCH A "BASEBALL" FROM A PLANE

Herman will always be synonymous with the Daffiness Dodgers of the late 1920s.

Career Highlights
Lifetime batting average: .324
181 home runs

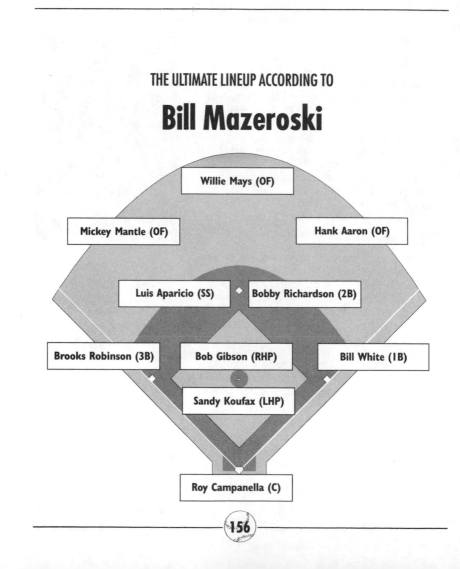

THE ULTIMATE LINEUP ACCORDING TO

Bill Mazeroski

Willie Mays (OF)

Mickey Mantle (OF)

Hank Aaron (OF)

Luis Aparicio (SS)

Bobby Richardson (2B)

Brooks Robinson (3B)

Bob Gibson (RHP)

Bill White (1B)

Sandy Koufax (LHP)

Roy Campanella (C)

MAZEROSKI WAS THE DOMINANT defensive second baseman in the National League for most of his 17 years with the Pirates (1956-72). A lifetime .260 hitter, he had exceptional power for a middle infielder, as evidenced by the fact that he hit home runs in double figures six times.

Mazeroski's single best year at the plate was probably 1962, when he hit .271 with 14 home runs, 24 doubles, and 81 runs batted in. He also holds the major league records for most double plays in a career (1,706) and in a single season (161). His single greatest moment on the diamond was his ninth-inning home run in the seventh game of the 1960 World Series against the Yankees that gave Pittsburgh a world championship.

According to Mazeroski, the era of the relief pitcher came too late for onetime teammate Elroy Face, and so he is one of the most underrated players of his time: "A lot of people mention me when the subject of underrated players come up, but I'll never understand how he has been ignored for so long. I guess it's a combination of having played in a relatively small city and coming out of the bullpen at a time when if you weren't a starter, you were considered second-rate. But even setting aside that phenomenal year (1959) when he was 18-1, here was a man who ended up with 104 wins, almost all of them from the bullpen, and who ended up leading the league in saves three times."

Mazeroski's legendary home run in the seventh game of the 1960 World Series against the Yankees won the Series for the Pirates.

Career Highlights
1,706 double plays
Lifetime batting average: .260

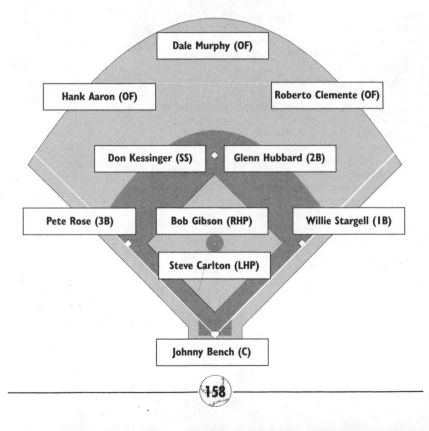

THE ULTIMATE LINEUP ACCORDING TO

Phil Niekro

Dale Murphy (OF)

Hank Aaron (OF)

Roberto Clemente (OF)

Don Kessinger (SS)

Glenn Hubbard (2B)

Pete Rose (3B)

Bob Gibson (RHP)

Willie Stargell (1B)

Steve Carlton (LHP)

Johnny Bench (C)

THE RIGHTHANDED Niekro spent the better part of his 24-year career with mostly undistinguished Braves teams in Milwaukee (1964-65) and Atlanta (1966-83). He later turned in productive seasons for the Yankees (1984-85) and tours with the Indians (1986-87) and Blue Jays (1987) before returning to the Braves (1987) for his final appearance at the age of 48. Overall, he won 318 and lost 274 with a 3.35 ERA, winning 20 or more three times (leading the National League once), hurling more than 300 innings four times (leading the league each time), and topping 200 strikeouts twice (leading National League hurlers once). He also paced the National League in ERA once.

Niekro's best seasons were probably 1969 (23-13, 2.57) and 1974 (20-13, 2.38), and his sole no-hitter came in 1973. He achieved his 300th victory on the final day of the 1985 season, avoiding his trademark knuckleball until the final pitch, a third strike on former teammate Jeff Burroughs.

Niekro's lineup leaves no room for Willie Mays, "because I only saw him at the end of his career, and Brooks Robinson, because we overlapped for such a brief time. Besides, Rose has to be in there somewhere. I played with Hubbard and I don't know anybody who was as quick around second base. Watching Kessinger make great plays against us over and over convinced me—or maybe he just had all of his great days against the Braves."

Niekro's toughest batter? "Rose got the most hits off me, but he faced me more than anyone else. I struck out Billy Buckner once in eight years. He always put the ball between the white lines, and that's the toughest guy to get out."

Career Highlights
318 wins
Lifetime ERA: 3.35

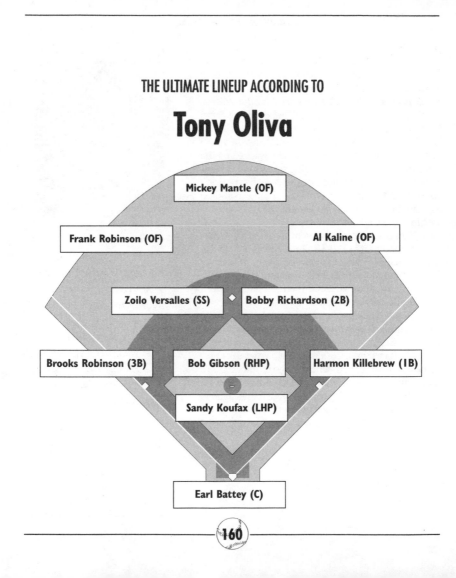

THE ULTIMATE LINEUP ACCORDING TO

Tony Oliva

Mickey Mantle (OF)

Frank Robinson (OF)

Al Kaline (OF)

Zoilo Versalles (SS)

Bobby Richardson (2B)

Brooks Robinson (3B)

Bob Gibson (RHP)

Harmon Killebrew (1B)

Sandy Koufax (LHP)

Earl Battey (C)

ONE OF THE DOMINANT HITTERS of his era, the lefthand-swinging Oliva batted .304 for the Twins in a 15-year career (1962-76) cut short by a bad knee. The American League's 1964 Rookie of the Year is the only player to win batting crowns in his first two full seasons (1964 and 1965), and in 1971 he added a third title.

Oliva also led the American League in slugging average in 1971, in hits five different seasons, and in doubles four times. His single best season was 1964, when he batted .323 with 32 home runs, 43 doubles, 94 runs batted in, and 109 runs scored. He also hit .440 in two American League Championship Series (1969 and 1970), knocking a home run and two doubles in each series.

Oliva regards Sam McDowell and Hoyt Wilhelm as his primary mound antagonists. "McDowell was big and wild and lefty, so you never knew what was coming and could never get comfortable at the plate. He was the direct opposite of Wilhelm, who threw a knuckleball on practically every pitch. That let you get comfortable, but he was still hard to hit."

Oliva sees onetime teammate Cesar Tovar as the most underrated player of his time. "Maybe you just had to be down on the field with him to appreciate how smooth he was and how much easier he made it for you to come to bat with him on base. He'd be the perfect tenth player on anybody's team."

MINNSEOTA TWINS   OUTFIELD

Oliva sees onetime teammate Cesar Tovar as the most underrated player of his time. "Maybe you just had to be down on the field with him to appreciate how smooth he was and how much easier he made it for you to come to bat with him on base."

Career Highlights
.304 batting average
Rookie of the Year: 1964
Batting Crowns: 1964, 1965, 1971

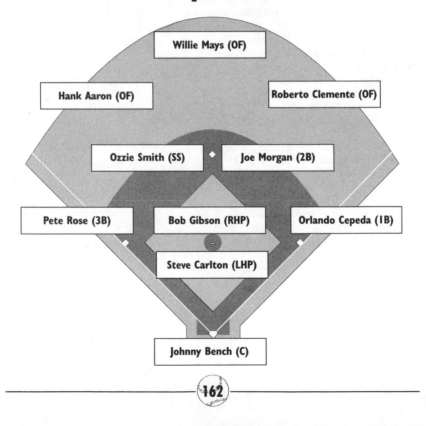

THE ULTIMATE LINEUP ACCORDING TO

Tony Perez

Willie Mays (OF)

Hank Aaron (OF)

Roberto Clemente (OF)

Ozzie Smith (SS)

Joe Morgan (2B)

Pete Rose (3B)

Bob Gibson (RHP)

Orlando Cepeda (1B)

Steve Carlton (LHP)

Johnny Bench (C)

PEREZ SPENT 23 SEASONS with the Reds (1964-76, 1984-86), Expos (1977-79), Red Sox (1980-82), and Phillies (1983). The righthanded hitter knocked home a minimum of 90 runs for 11 consecutive seasons (1967-77)—topping 100 runs batted in seven times in his career—and knocked 20 or more home runs nine times; he batted over .300 three times.

A third baseman-turned-first baseman, Perez concluded his career with a .279 average and 379 homers. His best season was 1970, when he achieved personal highs in batting (.317), homers (40), runs batted in (129), and runs scored (107). In the 1975 World Series, Perez hit three homers, the last of them in the seventh game off a bloop pitch thrown by Bill Lee.

Perez wanted himself among his lineup, because "I could win a game as much as anybody else. But I have to take myself off third and put Rose there. He has to be in the lineup somewhere, even though he had no position. And I can't put myself at first either. Cepeda would have to come before me. So would Willie McCovey, for that matter."

Like many contemporaries, Perez regards Gibson as his pitching nemesis. "His heater had two speeds—fast and unhittable—and I had trouble with both of them."

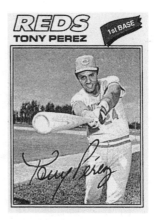

In the 1975 World Series, Perez hit three homers, the last of them in the seventh game off a bloop pitch thrown by Bill Lee.

Career Highlights
379 home runs
1,652 runs batted in

THE ULTIMATE LINEUP ACCORDING TO
Vada Pinson

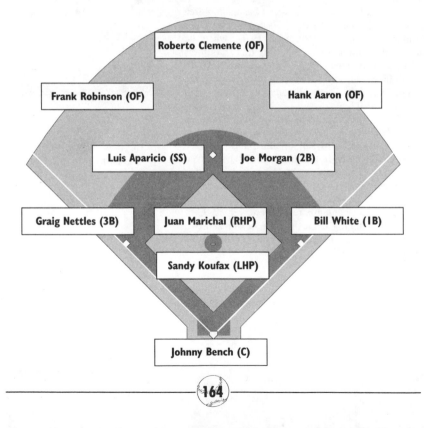

Roberto Clemente (OF)

Frank Robinson (OF)

Hank Aaron (OF)

Luis Aparicio (SS)

Joe Morgan (2B)

Graig Nettles (3B)

Juan Marichal (RHP)

Bill White (1B)

Sandy Koufax (LHP)

Johnny Bench (C)

PINSON BATTED .286 in 18 seasons for the Reds (1958-68), Cardinals (1969), Indians (1970-71), Angels (1972-73), and Royals (1974-75). While with the Reds, the lefty-hitting outfielder led the National League in hits in 1961 and 1963, in doubles in 1959 and 1960, in triples in 1963 and 1967, and in runs scored in 1959.

Pinson swatted at least 20 home runs in a season seven times, and drove in more than 100 runs twice. In 1961, his .343 mark was one of the main factors in Cincinnati's pennant win. He also had a career total of 305 stolen bases, swiping more than 20 in nine different seasons.

In Pinson's opinion, the most underrated player of his time was Curt Flood, who "had the misfortune of being in the league at the same time as Willie Mays, so every other center fielder was considered secondary. Plus, he didn't hit as many homers as Willie did. But for a day-in, day-out player who could hit, run, and catch the ball, he never got the credit he deserved for being the winner he was."

Vada Pinson

OUTFIELD CINCINNATI REDLEGS

Pinson's most difficult mound foes were "Marichal and Bob Gibson. They both kept you off balance all the time."

Career Highlights
256 home runs
305 stolen bases

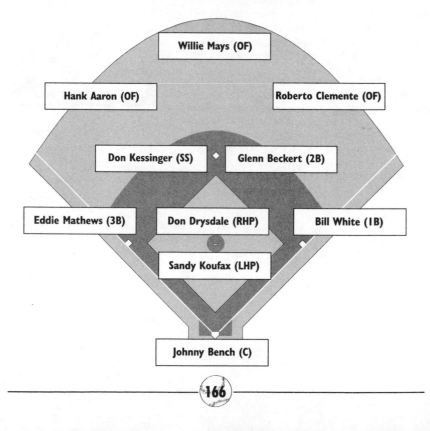

THE ULTIMATE LINEUP ACCORDING TO

Ron Santo

Willie Mays (OF)

Hank Aaron (OF)

Roberto Clemente (OF)

Don Kessinger (SS)

Glenn Beckert (2B)

Eddie Mathews (3B)

Don Drysdale (RHP)

Bill White (1B)

Sandy Koufax (LHP)

Johnny Bench (C)

SANTO, WHO RANKS FOURTH in home runs among all third baseman, was at the core of the Cubs offense from 1960 to 1973, winding up his career in 1974 with the White Sox. Regarded as an excellent fielder, the righthanded slugger hit 342 homers, topping the 20 mark 11 times, including four consecutive years of more than 30 (1964 through 1967). He also batted .300 or better four times, drove in more than 100 runs four times, and led the National League in walks four times and in triples once. His season highs were a .313 average in 1964, 33 homers in 1965, and 123 runs batted in in 1969.

As a footnote to his selections he adds: "Much as I'd like to find a place for Ernie Banks, it's no insult to say he wasn't the first baseman White was. And nobody could go into the hole as well as Kessinger. So Ernie is left without a position."

The most underrated player of his time, says Santo, is Ken Boyer. "He may be one of the few players whose stats show him to be much better than he was perceived as being when he was playing."

CHICAGO CUBS · 3rd BASE

Santo's toughest pitcher? "No one, really. To be able to hit is a gift and when the physical gift and the indefinable component come together on a given day, you can hit anybody. When they don't come together, you can't."

Career Highlights
Lifetime batting average: .277
342 home runs

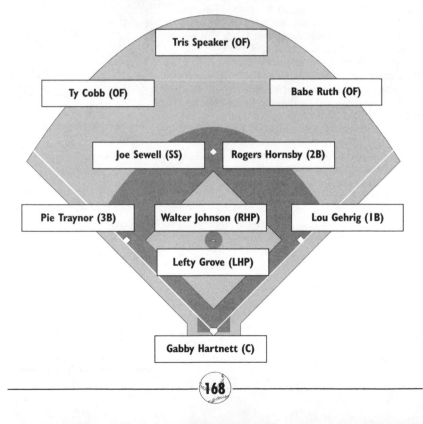

THE ULTIMATE LINEUP ACCORDING TO
Riggs Stephenson

Tris Speaker (OF)

Ty Cobb (OF)

Babe Ruth (OF)

Joe Sewell (SS)

Rogers Hornsby (2B)

Pie Traynor (3B)

Walter Johnson (RHP)

Lou Gehrig (1B)

Lefty Grove (LHP)

Gabby Hartnett (C)

STEPHENSON HAS THE HIGHEST batting average (.336) of any eligible player not in the Hall of Fame. The righthand-hitting outfielder spent five years as a general handyman for the Indians (1921-25) before moving over to the Cubs (1926-34), where he ripped off eight straight seasons in which he batted higher than .300. He led the National League with 46 doubles in 1927 and collected 49 two-baggers in 1932.

Stephenson's best season was 1929, when he hit .362 with 17 home runs, 36 doubles, 110 runs batted in, and 91 runs scored. That year, he formed—with Hack Wilson and Kiki Cuyler—the only outfield in National League history in which all three players had more than 100 runs batted in. In two World Series for Chicago, in 1929 and 1932, he hit a combined .378.

Stephenson never hesitated about his choice of the toughest pitcher: "Dazzy Vance pitched off a high mound and he was already a big man, so the ball came down at you instead of straight toward you. And his fastball would rise, too. He also had a sharp overhand curve, the kind we used to call a drop. Then, to make things even harder on the hitter, he'd cut his shirt around the right arm so you couldn't pick up the ball with those shreds of a sleeve flapping around."

RIGGS STEPHENSON
CHICAGO CUBS – OUTFIELD   1932

Stephenson has the highest batting average (.336) of any eligible player not in the Hall of Fame.

Career Highlights
Lifetime batting average: .336

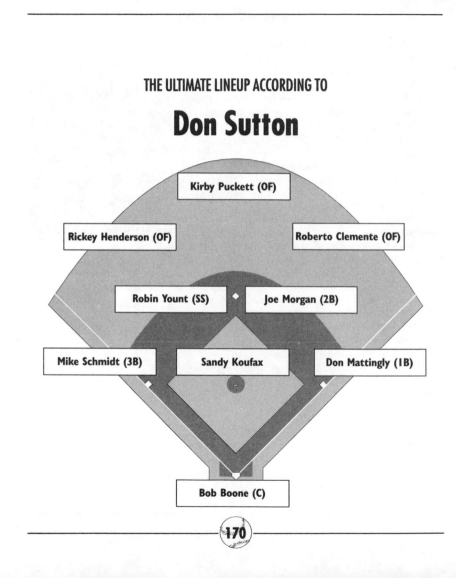

THE ULTIMATE LINEUP ACCORDING TO

Don Sutton

Kirby Puckett (OF)

Rickey Henderson (OF)

Roberto Clemente (OF)

Robin Yount (SS)

Joe Morgan (2B)

Mike Schmidt (3B)

Sandy Koufax

Don Mattingly (1B)

Bob Boone (C)

CONSISTENCY WAS THE HALLMARK of Sutton's 23-year career with the Dodgers (1966-80, 1988), Astros (1981-82), Brewers (1982-84), Athletics (1985), and Angels (1985-87). The righthander's career marks include a 324-256 record, a 3.26 ERA, 3,574 strikeouts (fifth on the all-time list), and 58 shutouts.

Although Sutton has the fewest 20-win seasons (only one) of any 300-game winner, he notched 15 or more victories per season 12 times. Similarly, he recorded more than 100 strikeouts in each of his first 21 seasons, topping 200 five times. He led the National League with a 2.21 ERA in 1980 and with nine shutouts in 1972, probably his best season (19-9, 2.08 ERA). His 230 victories in a Dodger uniform is the most by any Brooklyn or Los Angeles hurler.

Sutton explains his selections: "I tried to blend offense and defense. For example, Tommy Hutton was the best fielding first baseman I ever saw. And some of the big sluggers they put at first because they have to play somewhere couldn't catch a cold. Mattingly can do both. As for the pitcher, I only need one to win one game if that one is Koufax. I should add that Puckett may very well be the best player in baseball today. He may also be the nicest guy in baseball. It's hard not to beam in admiration even when he's kicking your butt."

Sutton's toughest opponents included Clemente, Bob Watson, and Bill Madlock. "But every time I faced Rance Mulliniks, I'd look up and he'd be standing at second or circling the bases. He always knew what was coming, so finally I gave up and told Bob Boone to tell him what I was going to throw."

DODGERS
DON SUTTON

"Every time I faced Rance Mulliniks, I'd look up and he'd be standing at second or circling the bases. He always knew what was coming, so finally I gave up and told Bob Boone to tell him what I was going to throw."

Career Highlights
324 wins
3,574 strikeouts
58 shutouts

And Finally . . .

Editor's Note:
While any sort of all-time all-star lineup is, of course, ultimately beyond determination, it is interesting to note where there is consensus among players of a particular era on the standout performers of that era. The authors began with the expressed intention of recording "knowledgeable evaluations of different periods in the evolution of twentieth-century baseball." The only player selected unanimously by contemporaries interviewed for this book (as well as by several non-contemporaries) was Honus Wagner. (Obviously, Wagner benefits from the fact that he was *the* standout shortstop of his era.) Beyond that, all else is the stuff of Hot Stove argument and speculation.

After all, if no one was able to resolve satisfactorily the Willie Mays–Mickey Mantle–Duke Snider debate of the 1950s, how much more difficult is it to weigh the relative merits of Tris Speaker and Joe DiMaggio or Sandy Koufax and Lefty Grove? Perhaps Tom Seaver had the final word on this matter when he told the authors that "when you are competing at that level of ability, the margins of difference aren't that great." While many more contemporaries picked Lou Gehrig than Jimmie Foxx, it is safe to conclude on the basis of their comments that none of them would find a Foxx-for-Gehrig substitution embarrassing. Nevertheless, if the opinions of teammates and rivals count for anything (and that is what the authors have recorded here), they yield the following distinctly unscientific, but decidedly potent, lineup.

First base: Lou Gehrig was named by slightly more than half of his contemporaries, far and away the best percentage of any first baseman.

Second base: Jackie Robinson was chosen by one fewer respondent than Charlie Gehringer, but the percentage of his contemporaries who named him was higher than that of the Detroit star.

Third base: Brooks Robinson beats out Pie Traynor with slightly more picks and a slightly higher percentage.

Shortstop: Honus Wagner was the unanimous choice of his contemporaries.

Outfield: Ty Cobb was selected by almost everyone who played with or against him.

Outfield: Willie Mays was picked for 25 lineups, the most of anyone.

Outfield: Babe Ruth is Babe Ruth—and is behind only Mays among position players in the number of lineups in which he appears.

Catcher: Johnny Bench, with 11 selections, beats out Roy Campanella, with the same number, because the percentage of contemporaries who chose the Cincinnati slugger was higher.

Righthanded pitcher: Walter Johnson edges Bob Gibson, because, while each was chosen an equal number of times, Johnson's entries represent a higher percentage of those who had to face him.

Lefthanded pitcher: Sandy Koufax has 21 nods, second only to Willie Mays's 25 among all players.

Baseball Card Credits

Hank Aaron, copyright The Topps Company, Inc. From the Collection of Bart Acocella.
Dick Allen, copyright The Topps Company, Inc. From the Collection of Bart Erbach.
Luis Aparicio, compliments of Glenn Stuart from Mr. Mint.
Luke Appling, reprinted with permission of Megacards, Inc., Fairfield, IA 52556 and The Sporting New Publishing Co., St. Louis, MO 63116.
Richie Ashburn, compliments of Glenn Stuart from Mr. Mint.
Ernie Banks, copyright The Topps Company, Inc. Compliments of Glenn Stuart from Mr. Mint.
Cool Papa Bell, compliments of Glenn Stuart from Mr. Mint.
Yogi Berra, copyright The Topps Company, Inc. From the collection of Bart Acocella.
Bobby Bonds, copyright the Topps Company, Inc. From the collection of Bart Acocella.
Lou Boudreau, compliments of Glenn Stuart from Mr. Mint.
George Brett, copyright The Topps Company, Inc. From the Collection of Bart Acocella.
Roy Campanella, compliments of Glenn Stuart from Mr. Mint.
Rod Carew, copyright The Topps Company, Inc. From the Collection of Bart Acocella.
Gary Carter, copyright The Topps Company, Inc. From the Collection of Bart Acocella.
Orlando Cepeda, copyright The Topps Company, Inc. Compliments of Glenn Stuart from Mr. Mint.
Fred Clarke, compliments of Glenn Stuart from Mr. Mint.
Ty Cobb, compliments of Glenn Stuart from Mr. Mint.
Mickey Cochrane, copyright The Topps Company, Inc. From the Collection of Bart Acocella.
Jocko Conlan, compliments of Glenn Stuart from Mr. Mint.
Sam Crawford, compliment of Glenn Stuart from Mr. Mint.
Bill Dickey, reprinted with permission of Megacards, Inc., Fairfield, IA 52556 and The Sporting News Publishing Co., St. Louis, MO 63116.
Bobby Doerr, reprinted with permission of Megacards, Inc., Fairfield, IA 52556 and The Sporting News Publishing Co., St. Louis, MO 63116.
Don Drysdale, copyright The Topps Company, Inc. From the Collection of Bart Erbach.
Bob Feller, reprinted with permission of Megacards, Inc., Fairfield, IA 52556, The Sporting News Publishing Co., St. Louis, MO 63116, and Curtis Management Group, Indianapolis, IN.
Rick Ferrell, compliments of Glenn Stuart from Mr. Mint.

Rollie Fingers, copyright The Topps Company, Inc. From the Collection of Bart Acocella.

Whitey Ford, copyright The Topps Company, Inc. (Bowman). Compliments of Glenn Stuart from Mr. Mint.

Charlie Gehringer, reprinted with permission of Megacards, Inc., Fairfield, IA 52556 and The Sporting News Publishing Co., St. Louis, MO 63116.

Bob Gibson, copyright The Topps Company, Inc. Compliments of Glenn Stuart from Mr. Mint.

Hank Greenberg, compliments of Glenn Stuart from Mr. Mint.

Burleigh Grimes, reprint with permission of Megacards, Inc., Fairfield, IA 52556 and The Sporting News Publishing Co., St. Louis, MO 63116.

Babe Herman, reprinted with permission of Megacards, Inc., Fairfield, IA 52556 and The Sporting News Publishing Co., St. Louis, MO 63116.

Billy Herman, reprinted with permission of Megacards, Inc., Fairfield, IA 52556 and The Sporting News Publishing Co., St. Louis, MO 63116.

Carl Hubbell, compliments of Glenn Stuart from Mr. Mint.

Monte Irvin, copyright The Topps Company, Inc. Compliments of Glenn Stuart from Mr. Mint.

Reggie Jackson, copyright The Topps Company, Inc. Compliment of Glenn Stuart from Mr. Mint.

Travis Jackson, reprinted with permission of Megacards, Inc., Fairfield, IA 52556 and The Sporting News Publishing Co., St. Louis, MO 63116.

Ferguson Jenkins, copyright The Topps Company, Inc. Compliments of Glenn Stuart from Mr. Mint.

Judy Johnson, National Baseball Library, Cooperstown, NY.

Al Kaline, copyright The Topps Company, Inc. Compliments of Glenn Stuart from Mr. Mint.

George Kell, compliments of Glenn Stuart from Mr. Mint.

Harmon Killebrew, copyright The Topps Company, Inc. Compliments of Glenn Stuart from Mr. Mint.

Ralph Kiner, copyright The Topps Company, Inc. From the Collection of Bart Acocella.

Nap Lajoie, compliments of Glenn Stuart from Mr. Mint.

Bob Lemon, copyright The Topps Company, Inc. Compliments of Glenn Stuart from Mr. Mint.

Buck Leonard, compliments of Glenn Stuart from Mr. Mint.

Al Lopez, reprinted with permission of Megacards, Inc., Fairfield, IA 52556 and The Sporting News Publishing Co., St. Louis, MO 63116.

Ted Lyons, reprinted with permission of Megacards, Inc., Fairfield, IA 52556 and The Sporting News Publishing Co., St. Louis, MO 63116.

Mickey Mantle, copyright The Topps Company, Inc. (Bowman). Compliments of Glenn Stuart from Mr. Mint.

Juan Marichal, copyright The Topps Company, Inc. From the Collection of Bart Erbach.

Eddie Mathews, compliments of Glenn Stuart from Mr. Mint.

Willie Mays, copyright The Topps Company, Inc. Compliments of Glenn Stuart from Mr. Mint.

Bill Mazeroski, copyright The Topps Company, Inc. Compliments of Glenn Stuart from Mr. Mint.

Willie McCovey, copyright The Topps Company, Inc. From the Collection of Bart Acocella.

Johnny Mize, reprinted with permission of Megacards, Inc., Fairfield, IA 52556 and The Sporting News Publishing Co., St. Louis, MO 63116, and Curtis Management Group, Indianapolis, IN.

Joe Morgan, copyright The Topps Company, Inc. Compliments of Glenn Stuart from Mr. Mint.

Hal Newhouser, reprinted with permission of Megacards, Inc., Fairfield, IA 52556 and The Sporting News Publishing Co., St. Louis, MO 63116.

Phil Niekro, copyright The Topps Company, Inc. From the Collection of Bart Acocella.

Tony Oliva, copyright The Topps Company, Inc. From the Collection of Bart Acocella.

Tony Perez, copyright The Topps Company, Inc. From the Collection of Bart Acocella.

Vada Pinson, copyright The Topps Company, Inc. Compliment of Glenn Stuart from Mr. Mint.

PeeWee Reese, copyright The Topps Company, Inc. Compliments of Glenn Stuart from Mr. Mint.

Phil Rizzuto, copyright The Topps Company, Inc. From the Collection of Bart Erbach.

Robin Roberts, compliments of Glenn Stuart from Mr. Mint.

Brooks Robinson, copyright The Topps Company, Inc. From the Collection of Bart Acocella.

Frank Robinson, copyright The Topps Company, Inc. Compliments of Glenn Stuart from Mr. Mint.

Edd Roush, reprinted with permission of Megacards, Inc., Fairfield, IA 52556 and The Sporting News Publishing Co., St. Louis, MO 63116, and Curtis Management Group, Indianapolis, IN.

Red Ruffing, reprinted with permission of Megacards, Inc., Fairfield, IA 52556 and The Sporting News Publishing Co., St. Louis, MO 63116.

Ron Santo, copyright The Topps Company, Inc. From the Collection of Bart Acocella.

Red Schoendienst, copyright The Topps Company, Inc. Compliments of Glenn Stuart from Mr. Mint.

Tom Seaver, copyright The Topps Company, Inc. From the Collection of Bart Acocella.

Joe Sewell, reprinted with permission of Megacards, Inc., Fairfield, IA 52556 and The Sporting News Publishing Co., St. Louis, MO 63116.

Enos Slaughter, reprinted with permission of Megacards, Inc., Fairfield, IA 52556 and The Sporting News Publishing Co., St. Louis, MO 63116, and Curtis Management Group, Indianapolis, IN.

Duke Snider, copyright The Topps Company, Inc. Compliments of Glenn Stuart from Mr. Mint.

Warren Spahn, compliments of Glenn Stuart from Mr. Mint.

Willie Stargell, copyright The Topps Company, Inc. From the Collection of Bart Acocella.

Riggs Stephenson, reprinted with permission of Megacards, Inc., Fairfield, IA 52556 and The Sporting News Publishing Co., St. Louis, MO 63116.

Don Sutton, copyright The Topps Company, Inc. From the Collection of Bart Acocella.

Bill Terry, reprinted with permission of Megacards, Inc., Fairfield, IA 52556 and The Sporting News Publishing Co., St. Louis, MO 63116.

Dazzy Vance, reprinted with permission of Megacards, Inc., Fairfield, IA 52556 and The Sporting News Publishing Co., St. Louis, MO 63116.

Billy Williams, copyright The Topps Company, Inc. Compliments of Glenn Stuart from Mr. Mint.

Ted Williams, copyright The Topps Company, Inc. (Bowman). Compliments of Glenn Stuart from Mr. Mint.

Early Wynn, copyright The Topps Company, Inc. Compliments of Glenn Stuart from Mr. Mint.

Cards reproduced with permission of Megacards are from *The Sporting News*® Conlon Collection™.

Index of Players and Managers